edition ♦ karo – verlag josefine rosalski 2013 – starke frauen

Bibliografische Information der Deutschen Nationalbibliothek:
Die Deutsche Nationalbibliothek verzeichnet diese Publikation in der
Deutschen Nationalbibliografie; detaillierte bibliografische Daten
sind im Internet über www.dnb.d-nb.de abrufbar.
Kirsten Liese, Wagnerheldinnen.
Berühmte Isolden und Brünnhilden aus einem Jahrhundert
Berlin 2013

1. Auflage
© edition ♦ karo im Verlag Josefine Rosalski, Berlin 2013
www.edition-karo.de
Übersetzung: Charles Scribner, New York; Annemarie Hanauer (Assistenz), Melle
Druck und Verarbeitung: SDL Digitaler Buchdruck, Berlin
Gedruckt in Deutschland
ISBN 978-3-937881-62-1

Kirsten Liese

Wagnerheldinnen

Wagnerian Heroines

Berühmte Isolden und Brünnhilden aus einem Jahrhundert

A Century of Great Isoldes and Brünnhildes

Verlag Josefine Rosalski, Berlin 2013

Für meine Eltern
und meine Freundin Jacqueline

For my parents, and for my dear friend Jacqueline

Inhaltsverzeichnis / Table of Contents

Geleitwort

von Christian Thielemann

Martha Mödl hat einmal gesagt: »Es ist das größte Glück für eine Hochdramatische, Isolde und Brünnhilde singen zu *dürfen*.«

So haben es vermutlich alle großen Kolleginnen empfunden, die mit diesen Figuren Geschichte schrieben, auch wenn die eine oder andere sicherlich Fürchterliches durchgemacht hat, bedenkt man, welch hohe Ansprüche diese Partien stellen, nervlich, physisch und mental! Für mich persönlich ist der *Tristan* eine gefährliche Droge, weil er in uns Gefühle weckt, die wir nicht mehr abschalten können und die keine Grenze kennen. Das macht Angst, und das ist der Grund dafür, warum ich dieses Werk nicht so oft dirigieren kann beziehungsweise immer große Abstände zwischen den Produktionen benötige. Wenn ich bedenke, wie viele Male dagegen Kirsten Flagstad, Martha Mödl, Astrid Varnay, Catarina Ligendza, Birgit Nilsson, Gwyneth Jones, Deborah Polaski oder auch Waltraud Meier – um nur einige hervorzuheben – die Isolde mit äußerster Hingabe verkörpert haben, dann verschlägt mir das den Atem.

All diese Heroinen, die diesen großen Tragödinnen rundum gerecht wurden und werden, haben diese Würdigung verdient. Eine Hommage, die auch eine verdienstvolle ist, denn anhand dieser Biographien vermittelt sich zugleich, was nötig ist, damit sich eine Stimme so prächtig entwickeln kann. So rasant, wie heute oftmals Sängerkarrieren forciert werden, muss man sich kaum wundern, dass es im hochdramatischen Fach derzeit nicht allzu viele Kräfte dieser Klasse gibt.

In diesem Sinne hoffe ich, dass diese kleine Monographie auch dazu anspornt, den hier versammelten Persönlichkeiten nachzueifern.

Christian Thielemann

Foreword

by Christian Thielemann

Martha Mödl once said: »A Wagnerian soprano's greatest joy is to be allowed to sing Isolde or Brünnhilde.«

Great peers of hers, who themselves made history performing these two roles, probably felt the same awe, considering the mental and physical tolls they had to endure. For me, *Tristan* is like a dangerous drug: it elicits powerful feelings that cannot be turned off and know no limits. It is a frightening experience indeed, and this is the reason why I feel unable to conduct *Tristan* too frequently. I need a lot of time between productions. It therefore takes my breath away to recall how often Kirsten Flagstad, Martha Mödl, Astrid Varnay, Catarina Ligendza, Birgit Nilsson, Gwyneth Jones, Deborah Polaski as well as Waltraud Meier – to mention only a few – sang Isolde with the utmost dedication.

Each and every heroine who did and still does justice to the great Wagnerian soprano roles deserves this appraisal, a homage based on merit alone. The biographies assembled in this book prove how much time and work are required for a voice to develop its splendor. Given the accelerated pace of contemporary singing careers, it is hardly surprising that only a few Wagnerian sopranos of this class are still with us.

In this spirit, I hope this little monograph will encourage readers to emulate the great women it portrays.

Christian Thielemann

Einleitung

Stolz, klug, schön und kühn: Isolde und Brünnhilde sind faszinierende Persönlichkeiten und, wie die meisten Frauenfiguren in Wagners Musikdramen, stark in ihrer Liebe. Sie stellen in jeder Hinsicht hohe Ansprüche an ihre Interpretinnen, denen dieses Buch gewidmet ist.

Meine Sammlung erhebt indes nicht den Anspruch eines Nachschlagewerks, versteht sich vielmehr als eine persönliche Auslese repräsentativer Vertreterinnen unterschiedlicher Epochen, mit denen ich mich seit frühester Jugend, später auch als Journalistin, intensiver beschäftigt habe. – Ich bin sehr dankbar, die meisten darunter auf der Bühne erlebt zu haben.

Waltraud Meier ist die einzige Sängerin in diesem Buch, die nur die Isolde in ihrem Repertoire hat, nicht aber die Brünnhilde. Ich wollte jedoch auf keinen Fall auf sie verzichten, da sie mit ihrer großartigen musikalischen Gestaltung und ihrer sagenhaften Bühnenpräsenz aus der jüngeren Aufführungsgeschichte des *Tristans* nicht wegzudenken ist. Viele Male habe ich sie als Isolde in Berlin und in München bewundert.

Unvergessen sind mir vor allem zahlreiche Wagnerproduktionen an der Deutschen Oper Berlin in ihrer erfolgreichsten Ära der 1970er und 80er Jahre. Das Haus steht in einer langen Wagnertradition und ist den Bayreuther Festspielen sehr eng verbunden. Nahezu alle Sängergrößen der damaligen Zeit haben hier gastiert, trotz erschwerter Reisebedingungen in der damals noch geteilten Stadt. Es waren allen voran Catarina Ligendza und Dame Gwyneth Jones, die als herrliche Isolden und Brünnhilden in stimmungsvollen Inszenierungen von Götz Friedrich meine Faszination für den *Tristan* und die *Ring*-Tetralogie weckten.

Solche Eindrücke und Erinnerungen sind für mich sehr entscheidend, da mich neben den musikalischen Qualitäten immer auch die Persönlichkeit einer Sängerin interessiert.

Unter den historischen Wagnerheldinnen nimmt meine Namensschwester Kirsten Flagstad eine Sonderstellung bei mir ein, da meine Eltern mich nach ihr benannt haben.

Als Berlinerin ist es mir natürlich auch eine Ehrensache, eine Größe vorzustellen, deren Geschichte eng mit meiner Heimatstadt verbunden ist: Frida Leider wurde in Berlin geboren, sie schrieb an der Staatsoper ab den frühen 1920er Jahren entscheidend bis zum Ende ihrer Karriere Aufführungsgeschichte und hat auch in Berlin ihre letzte Ruhe gefunden.

Die berühmte Nachkriegsheroine Martha Mödl ist mir ebenfalls seit Jugendzeiten ein Begriff. Umso mehr bedaure ich es, dass ich diese außergewöhnliche Künstlerin, die noch bis ins hohe Alter in kleinsten Rollen ein Ereignis war, auf der Bühne nicht erlebt habe. Irgendwie hat es sich nicht ergeben. Und doch hat es das Schicksal gewollt, dass ich mich just mit ihr in den vergangenen Jahren ganz besonders beschäftigen sollte. Ich verdanke dies meiner Begegnung mit Helmut Vetter, der eng mit ihr befreundet war, ihren Nachlass verwaltet, und noch immer höchst engagiert das Andenken an sie bewahrt. In die Edition *Martha Mödl – The Portrait of a Legend*, die von Fachzeitschriften 2012 als *CD des Jahres* ausgezeichnet wurde, hat er mich vertrauensvoll als Booklet-Autorin eingebunden, wofür ich ihm sehr dankbar bin!

Vetter war es auch, der die persönliche Verbindung zu Ludmila Dvořáková herstellte, die wie Frida Leider Berliner Operngeschichte schrieb.

Bei den historischen Sängerinnen war ich freilich auf Tondokumente, Selbstauskünfte, Erinnerungen von Angehörigen, Freunden, Weggefährten oder Verbänden sowie auf Rezensionen angewiesen. Die Materiallage war dabei ein weiteres Auswahlkriterium für die Namen in diesem Buch: Ich wollte mir nicht anmaßen, eine Künstlerin zu porträtieren, von der ich kaum mehr in Erfahrung bringen kann als die Eckdaten ihrer Karriere.

Insgesamt waren die 1920er bis 60er Jahre derart reich mit herrlichen Stimmen gesegnet, wie es sie wohl so zahlreich nie wieder geben wird. Leider, Flagstad, Mödl, Varnay und Nilsson, die ich in den folgenden Kapiteln vorstelle, waren große Säulen in diesem Arsenal. Darüber hinaus aber gab es zahlreiche weitere hervorragende Brünnhilden und Isolden, von Nanny Larsén-Todsen, Martha Fuchs oder Gertrude Kappel über Marjorie Lawrence und Germaine Lubin bis hin zu Gertrude Grob-Prandl.

Sehr zu Unrecht vergessen wurde vor allem auch die Amerikanerin Helen Traubel (1898-1972), der an dieser Stelle einige Zeilen gewidmet seien. Der Stimmenexperte Jens Malte Fischer nennt sie zu Recht eine der »prachtvollsten Wagner-Stimmen, die es je gegeben hat, [...] und eine fast ebenbürtige Konkurrentin Kirsten Flagstads.« Plattenaufnahmen bestätigen diesen Eindruck, wird hier doch eine in allen Registern perfekt geführte, kraftvolle, sinnlich leuchtende Stimme hörbar.

Leider sang Helen Traubel ausschließlich in Amerika, weshalb sie in Europa weniger bekannt wurde. Zudem nahm die turbulente Karriere dieser Künstlerin, die nebenher auch Krimis schrieb, einen abrupten Ausklang: Der kapriziöse damalige Met-Intendant Rudolf Bing verlängerte 1953 ihren Vertrag nicht, weil sie seit dem Zweiten Weltkrieg zunehmend auch in Operetten, Musicals und Fernsehshows auftrat.

Sympathisch nimmt Astrid Varnay die Kollegin in ihren Memoiren gegenüber dem strengen Chef in Schutz: »Mr. Bing schien den Eindruck zu haben, dass das Gelächter, das Helen Traubel im Fernsehen [...] einheimste, und das ansteckende Lachen, das sie selbst

14

immer wieder losließ, der Sache der Oper irgendwie schadeten, während sie damit in Wirklichkeit mehr Kunden an die Kasse lockte, als das künstliche Gezicke des Managements für sich in Anspruch nehmen konnte.«

Wie zufrieden war nun Richard Wagner mit den Isolden und Brünnhilden seiner Zeit? – Die größte Verehrung des Komponisten galt bekanntlich der Sopranistin Wilhelmine Schröder-Devrient, die ihn mit ihrer dramatischen Kunst als *Fidelio* aufs Höchste entzückte und drei seiner Figuren in den Uraufführungen verkörperte: den Adriano im *Rienzi*, die Senta im *Fliegenden Holländer* und die Venus im *Tannhäuser*. Für seine hochdramatischen Partien stand sie jedoch nicht mehr zur Verfügung, sie starb 1860.

Helen Traubel als Isolde

So wie Wagner mit seinem dramatischen Gesangsstil Neuland betrat, gab es nur wenige Sängerinnen und Sänger, die sich seinen Ansprüchen gewachsen zeigten. Das wurde vor allem schmerzlich offenbar bei dem Versuch, den *Tristan* einzustudieren. Seine Uraufführung am 10. Juni 1865 an der Münchner Hofoper ist eine Pioniertat ohnegleichen. Viele Anstrengungen, das Liebesdrama in Karlsruhe oder in Wien auf die Bühne zu bringen, waren zuvor fatal gescheitert. Vor allem die Besetzung der männlichen Titelpartie erwies sich dabei als eine große Hürde.

In Wien ließ sich der Tenor Alois Ander oft schwer erkältet bei den Proben entschuldigen und hatte beim Studium des zweiten Akts den ersten wohl schon wieder vergessen.

Ludwig und Malvina Schnorr von Carolsfeld als Tristan und Isolde

Über die Sopranistin Marie Louise Dustmann-Meyer, die in Wien die Isolde singen sollte, äußerte sich Wagner in seinen Briefen dagegen durchaus zuversichtlich: Sie kenne bereits »ihre Rolle und singt sie bewunderungswürdig«, schrieb der Komponist im November 1861 an den befreundeten französischen Schriftsteller Charles de Lorbac in Paris.

Am Ende aber scheiterte der *Tristan* nach mehr als 70 (!) Proben in Wien und galt als »unaufführbar«.

Erst nachdem der Bayernkönig Ludwig II. Wagner nach München geholt hatte, konnte ein weiterer

Anlauf riskiert werden. Es waren nun der von Wagner hoch verehrte Ludwig Schnorr von Carolsfeld und seine Frau Malvina, die sich mutig den großen Herausforderungen stellten und den Komponisten sehr zufrieden stimmten.

So schrieb Wagner über die Probenarbeit in München: »Zum erstenmal in meinem Leben war ich hier mit meiner ganzen, vollen Kunst wie auf einem Pfühl der Liebe gebettet. So musste es einmal sein! Edel, groß, frei und reich die Anlage der ganzen Kunstwerkstatt,

ein wunderbar, vom Himmel mir beschiedenes Künstlerpaar, innig vertraut und liebevollst ergeben, begabt zum Erstaunen […] Wie ein Zaubertraum wuchs das Werk zur ungeahnten Wirklichkeit: die erste Aufführung – ohne Publikum, nur für uns – als Generalprobe ausgegeben (11. Mai 1865!), glich der Erfüllung des Unmöglichen.«

Dame Gwyneth Jones bei ihrer Hommage *Oh Malvina*

Dame Gwyneth Jones hat die Pionierin Malvina in einem vierstündigen Wagnerfilm an der Seite von Richard Burton verkörpert. Sie hat dieser bemerkenswerten Frau Anfang der 1990er Jahre auch zusammen mit dem Journalisten Klaus Geitel ein wunderbares musikalisches Denkmal unter dem Titel *Oh Malvina* gesetzt, eine Lesung mit musikalischen Einlagen: »Die Technik des Belcanto transportierte bei ihr wohl nicht gerade das, was man *una bella voce* nennt«, heißt es da über Malvina im Text, »eine Engelsstimme war die ihre wohl nicht. Aber das hat man ja selbst in unseren kritischen Tagen nicht von jeder Tigerin des Singens erwartet.«

Nur eine einzige Äußerung konnte ich von Richard Wagner zu der Sopranistin Sophie Stehle finden, seiner Brünnhilde in der Münchner Uraufführung der *Walküre* am 26. Juni 1870: »Die Stehle ist sehr gut, unverdorbene Stimme und Manier«, schreibt er an den Dirigenten Hans von Bülow.

Ganz besonders begeistert war Wagner offenbar auch von Amalie Materna, der Brünnhilde seines ersten *Ring*-Zyklus' in Bayreuth. An sie schreibt er 1876, einige Wochen nach der Uraufführung seiner *Götterdämmerung*: »Mein liebes, theures Wesen! Treueste aller Getreuen! Lob, Ruhm, Ehre und Liebe vor allen Ihnen, meine tapfere Brünnhilde! Sie waren die Beste und Vertrauteste, die nur dem einen lebte, nie wankte, muthig, fest und heiter von Gelingen zu Gelingen vorwärts schritt!« Und am

Amalie Materna

13. November 1878 schreibt er: »Nur ein Wort der Erinnerung und der nachlebenden Freude daran, daß ich in Ihnen Eine von denen gewinnen durfte, denen ich wirklich etwas lehren konnte! Die Treue und Echtheit Ihrer Wiedergabe unserer Brünnhilde ist eines der für mich werthvollsten Zeugnisse dafür, daß für meine Kunst noch etwas zu hoffen ist.«

Auch die legendäre Würzburgerin Lilli Lehmann (1848-1929) hatte Richard Wagner noch persönlich kennen gelernt. Auf seinen Wunsch hin sang sie 1876 im ersten Bayreuther *Ring* kleinere Partien wie Woglinde, Helmwige und die Stimme des Waldvogels. 20 Jahre später stieg sie zu einer führenden hochdramatischen Sopranistin auf und verkörperte in Bayreuth die Brünnhilde.

Heute nun ist der Bedarf an Aufführungen des *Tristans* und des *Rings* größer denn je, vor allem zum Wagnerjahr 2013 verschreiben sich viele Bühnen ehrgeizigen Projekten, darunter zunehmend auch kleinere ambitionierte Häuser. Nur fehlen ihnen die geeigneten Sänger dazu, an herausragenden Kräften herrscht ein eklatanter Mangel wie zu Wagners Lebzeiten. Viele Soprane tönen sehr scharf in den Spitzen und flackern unschön in den Höhen.

Die großartige Nina Stemme ist eine der wenigen Ausnahmen, sie versteht ihre Stimme in allen Registern schlank zu führen.

Eine große Hoffnung am Himmel der Hochdramatischen ist die Frankfurterin Petra Lang, die gerade die Brünnhilde in ihr Repertoire aufgenommen hat. Bei ihrem Debüt in der *Walküre* des konzertanten Wagner-Zyklus von Marek Janowski konnte ich sie in der Berliner Philharmonie erleben und mich davon überzeugen, dass diese auch äußerlich sehr attraktive Frau alles besitzt, was eine exzellente Brünnhilde ausmacht.

Stimmliche Vorlieben sind zweifellos subjektiv. Über das Timbre einer Sängerin lässt sich nicht streiten, es ist eine Frage des Geschmacks. So ist es auch ganz natürlich, wenn die Meinungen über die in diesem Buch versammelten Heldinnen auseinander gehen.

Ich hoffe gleichwohl, dass mein kleiner Streifzug durch ein Jahrhundert des Wagnergesangs dazu anregt, meine Isolden und Brünnhilden – je nach Verfügbarkeiten – in Ton- oder Videoaufnahmen erleben zu wollen, im Idealfall freilich live auf der Bühne. Am Ende staunt man über immense Unterschiede der Interpretationen und Rollengestaltungen, und jede überzeugt auf ihre Weise. Indirekt ist das wohl auch ein Beweis für die Zeitlosigkeit dieser beiden so faszinierenden, komplexen Frauenfiguren und für die Genialität Richard Wagners.

Introduction

Proud, clever, beautiful and bold: Isolde and Brünnhilde are fascinating personalities and, like most female roles in Wagner's music dramas, intense in their love. In every respect they demand high standards of their performers, to whom this book is devoted.

My collection of Wagnerian sopranos does not claim to be a reference book, but rather a personal selection of eminent representatives from various eras. From my early youth onward as a journalist, I have immersed myself in their careers and lives. I am very grateful to have experienced most of them live on stage.

Waltraud Meier is the only performer in this book whose repertoire includes Isolde but not Brünnhilde. Yet I could by no means omit her from the roster in view of her magnificent musicality and fabulous stage presence that make *Tristan*'s recent performance history unimaginable without her. I have often marveled at her Isolde in Berlin and Munich.

I have been especially impressed by so many Wagnerian productions at the Deutsche Oper Berlin throughout its most successful era of the 1970s and 80s. That house boasts a long Wagnerian tradition and is closely linked to the Bayreuth Festival. Almost all the great performers of that time made guest appearances here despite the logistical hurdles during the years of the Berlin Wall. Above all, it was the brilliant Isoldes of Catarina Ligendza and Dame Gwyneth Jones in those atmospheric productions by Götz Friedrich that sparked my enthusiasm for *Tristan* and the *Ring* cycle.

Such impressions and memories are crucial for me, since I am not interested in sheer musical qualities alone, but always in the distinct personality of each singer.

Among the historic Wagnerian heroines my namesake Kirsten Flagstad occupies a special place, since my parents named me after her.

As a Berliner, moreover, I naturally consider it an honor to present a great performer whose story is closely linked to my hometown: Frida Leider was born in Berlin, made performance history at the Staatsoper from the early 1920s until the end of her career, and was laid to rest in Berlin.

The famous post-war heroine Martha Mödl has been a household name for me ever since my youth. Even in the smallest roles in her late years she was a phenomenon. I regret all the more that I never saw this extraordinary artist on stage. It was not to be. Yet as fate would have it, I was to be professionally engaged with her in recent years – something I owe to my meeting with Helmut Vetter, who was a close friend of hers, administers her estate, and remains dedicated to perpetuating her memory. In *Martha Mödl – A Portrait of a Legend*, which was named CD of the year in 2012 by professional music journals, he entrusted me to write the accompanying booklet, a commission I greatly appreciate!

Vetter also introduced me to Ludmila Dvořáková, who like Frida Leider made opera history in Berlin.

For the earlier legendary performers I was admittedly dependent on recordings, self-disclosures, recollections of relatives, friends, companions or organizations, as well as reviews. Available material was another criterion for selecting the names in this book: I did not want to presume to present an artist about whom I could learn little more than the bare outlines of her career.

All in all, the era from the 1920s through the 60s was blessed with superb voices in an abundance that will probably never be equaled. Leider, Flagstad, Mödl, Varnay and Nilsson, whom I present in the following chapters, were great pillars in this arsenal. In addition to these, there were many other outstanding Brünnhildes and Isoldes: Nanny Larsén-Todsen, Martha Fuchs, Gertrude Kappel, Marjorie Lawrence, Germaine Lubin and Gertrude Grob-Prandl.

It is so unjust that the American soprano Helen Traubel (1898-1972) tends to be overlooked. At this stage some lines must be devoted to her. The musicologist Jens Malte Fischer justifiably calls her one of the »most magnificent Wagnerian voices ever […], an almost equal rival to Kirsten Flagstad.« The recordings confirm this impression, since they display a perfectly controlled, powerful, bright, sensual voice through all registers.

Unfortunately, Helen Traubel sang exclusively in America, which is why she was less famous in Europe. This artist, who also wrote mystery novels, had a turbulent career with an abrupt end: the capricious general manager of the Met, Rudolf Bing, did not renew her contract in 1953, because she increasingly appeared in operettas, musicals and television shows after World War II.

In her memoirs, Astrid Varnay sympathetically comes to Traubel's defense against her stern boss: »Mr. Bing seemed to have the impression that the laughter Traubel provoked on television […], along with her own infectious laugh, would somehow hurt the opera, whereas she actually attracted more paying customers than management with its silly fuss over it could ask for.«

How pleased was Richard Wagner with the Isoldes and Brünnhildes of his day? The composer's adoration of the soprano Wilhelmine Schröder-Devrient is well known. She delighted him with her dramatic powers as *Fidelio* and debuted three of his own roles: Adriano in

Rienzi, Senta in *The Fying Dutchman* and Venus in *Tannhäuser*. Unfortunately she was not to be at hand for his later highly dramatic roles since she died in 1860.

As Wagner broke new ground with his dramatic style of singing, there were but few performers who could meet these requirements – a fact that became painfully obvious in the attempts to stage *Tristan*. The premiere on 10 June 1865 at the Munich Court Opera House was a pioneering feat without precedent. Several previous efforts to stage that romantic drama in Karlsruhe and Vienna proved disastrous failures. Above all, casting the male lead posed a huge challenge.

In Vienna, Alois Ander often missed rehearsals owing to severe colds, and then while studying for the second act had already forgotten the first. Wagner, however, is outspoken in his confidence in the soprano Marie Louise Dustmann-Meyer, who was to sing Isolde in Vienna: She already knows »her role and sings it admirably«, the composer writes in November 1861 to his friend the French author Charles de Lorbac in Paris.

In the end, *Tristan* flopped after over 70 (!) rehearsals in Vienna and was considered »unperformable«.

Only after Ludwig II, king of Bavaria, brought Wagner to Munich could they risk another attempt. Now Ludwig Schnorr von Carolsfeld, much admired by Wagner, and his wife Malvina bravely met the challenge and won the composer over.

As Wagner wrote about the rehearsals in Munich: »The first time in my life I was here with my entire, complete art embedded on a cushion of love. It was bound to happen once! How noble, huge, free and rich is the talent of the whole studio. Heaven has granted me a wonderful artistic couple: deeply intimate, tenderly devoted, and astonishingly talented […] Like a magic dream the work grew into unimagined reality: the first performance – without audience, just for us – was the dress rehearsal (11th May, 1865!); it was like the realization of the impossible.«

Dame Gwyneth Jones played the pioneering Malvina in a four-hour movie about Wagner starring Richard Burton. Together with journalist Klaus Geitel she also presented at the beginning of the 1990s a wonderful musical memorial to this distinguished woman under the title *O Malvina*, a dramatic reading with musical interludes: »The *bel canto* technique did not convey what one calls *una bella voce*« – so reads the text about Malvina: »She did not have an angel's voice. However, even in our own day critics do not expect it from every vocal tigress.«

I could find only a single comment by Richard Wagner about the soprano Sophie Stehle, his Brünnhilde at the Munich premiere of *Die Walküre* on 26 June 1870: »Stehle is very good, with her pristine voice and style«, he wrote to the conductor Hans von Bülow.

Wagner was just as openly enthusiastic about Amalie Materna, who sang Brünnhilde in his first *Ring* Cycle at Bayreuth. He writes to her in 1876, some weeks after the premiere of *Götterdämmerung*: »My lovely, dear one! Most faithful of the faithful! Praise, fame, honor and love for you above all, my valiant Brünnhilde! You were the best and most trustworthy who ever lived for one man alone – never wavering, brave, strong and cheerful, you strode from success to success!« Then on 13 November 1878 he wrote: »Just a word of reminder and lasting delight that I was allowed to find in you the one to whom I could truly teach something! The fidelity and authenticity of your Brünnhilde is to me one of the most precious testimonials that there is still hope for my art.«

The legendary Lilli Lehmann (1848-1929) from Würzburg also met Wagner in person. At his request, she sang in the first Bayreuth *Ring* in 1876 such smaller roles as Woglinde, Helmwige and the voice of the Woodbird. Twenty years later she was one of the leading Wagnerian sopranos and sang Brünnhilde at Bayreuth.

Today the demand for *Tristan* and *Ring* performances is greater than ever. Above all, for the Wagner Bicentennial in 2013 many opera companies – including smaller aspiring houses – have committed themselves to ambitious projects. The only dearth is in qualified singers – a glaring lack of outstanding talent as in Wagner's own lifetime. So many sopranos sound strident in their high notes, with an unpleasant wobbling in the upper register.

The brilliant Nina Stemme is one of the few exceptions. She knows how to focus her voice in all registers.

Among Wagnerian sopranos, Petra Lang from Frankfurt raises high hopes. She recently included Brünnhilde in her repertory. At her debut in *Die Walküre* during the *Ring* Cycle in concert under Marek Janowski with the Berlin Philharmonic, I was convinced that this very attractive woman has everything needed to be an excellent Brünnhilde.

Vocal preferences are surely subjective. One cannot reasonably argue about a singer's timbre: it is a matter of taste. It is thus only natural that opinions will differ over the heroines assembled in this book.

Nevertheless, I hope that my brief survey through this century of Wagnerian heroines may kindle the desire to experience for oneself my Isoldes and Brünnhildes – as available via audio or video recordings or, ideally, live on stage. In the end, one can but marvel at the vast differences among interpretations and characterizations, each in its own way convincing. Perhaps this is implicit proof of both the timelessness of these fascinating, complex heroines and of Wagner's genius.

Frida Leider, *18. April 1888 in Berlin

Flügelhelme, echte Pferde und lodernde Scheiterhaufen: Die Ära der 1920er und 30er Jahre, in der Frida Leider zu einer der bedeutendsten Wagnerheroinen aufsteigt, ist geprägt von einem großen, realistischen Theaterzauber, der schon im Neu-Bayreuth Wieland Wagners kaum noch denkbar scheint. Noch tragen die Brünnhilden bei der *Todesverkündigung* eine bleischwere Rüstung: »Helm und Panzer, Schild und Speer waren kaum zu heben«, schreibt Frida Leider in ihren Memoiren, »im wahrsten Sinne des Wortes sang ich: *Schwer wiegt mir der Waffen Wucht.*« [1]

Vor allem die sehr naturalistischen *Götterdämmerungen* in der Waldoper Zoppot bedeuten für die Sopranistin szenisch eine zusätzliche Prüfung: »Zu gerne knabberte Grane (Brünnhildes Ross) an meiner Perücke, wobei es noch mit dem Fuß scharrte, was natürlich eine Bitte um Zucker bedeutet. Aber ich war weiß Gott mit anderen Dingen beschäftigt und immer froh, wenn das Pferd einigermaßen ruhig stand. [...] Während der Scheiterhaufen lichterloh brannte, stand in der Laubkulisse ein Polizist im Brünnhilden-Kostüm mit Perücke, schwang sich auf das Pferd und sprang mit einem tollkühnen Satz über den brennenden Scheiterhaufen.« [2]

Frida Leider wird zu Recht oft als die Vollkommenste unter den Hochdramatischen im Wagnerfach gewürdigt. Noch in den höchsten Spitzen leuchtet ihr Sopran kraftvoll-majestätisch, bei den Übergängen zwischen den Registern vernimmt man nicht den geringsten Bruch, ihre Stimme klingt stets dunkel, klar und schön. So sehen das auch Kritiker. »Wie sicher und vornehm wird der Ton erfasst und gebildet, wie melodisch gelingt die Bildung der Töne«, begeistert sich etwa 1932 die *Wiener Zeitung*. [3]

Die Sopranistin interpretiert ihre Wagnerpartien im Belcanto-Stil: »Ich studierte Wagner sehr genau auf seine dynamischen Vorschriften und kam allmählich zu der Erkenntnis, dass meine Gesangstechnik und Richard Wagners Anforderungen bestimmt zu einem künstlerischen Resultat führen mussten.« [4]

Fridas Talent fällt zwar schon früh in der Schule auf, doch für ein Gesangsstudium fehlt zunächst das Geld. In einer Zeit, in der sich Frauen noch langsam aber zäh einen Weg in die Männerberufe bahnen, zählt Frida Leider zu den ersten, die einen kaufmännischen Beruf ergreifen. Gesangsstunden nimmt sie privat nebenher.

Zur entscheidenden Wende kommt es, als sie kurz vor Ausbruch des Ersten Weltkriegs für den Chor der Königlichen Oper Berlin vorsingt. Der Leiter erkennt ihr dramatisches Potenzial und rät ihr, sich unbedingt als Solistin ausbilden zu lassen. Im Zuge dessen nimmt nun die Mutter eine Stellung in einem Büro an, so kann sich Frida voll und ganz auf das Singen konzentrieren.

Ihre ersten Engagements führen die Sopranistin an kleinere Bühnen nach Halle, Rostock und Königsberg, 1919 kommt sie in Hamburg erstmals an ein großes Haus. Als sich 1923 der lang gehegte Traum von einem festen Engagement an der Berliner Staatsoper erfüllt, ist Frida Leider 35 Jahre alt, technisch blendend gerüstet, belastbar, im Szenischen gereift und somit bereit für eine Weltkarriere.

Es ist immer wieder die Isolde, die ihr in den entscheidenden Momenten Glück bringt. Schon Anfang der 1920er Jahre prophezeit ihr der Hamburger Intendant Löwenfeld begeistert, er mache die größte Isolde aller Zeiten aus ihr. Später debütiert sie in dieser Rolle in London und an der New Yorker Met, wo sie große Triumphe feiert.

Leiders schönste Erinnerung gilt einer *Tristan*-Aufführung an der Berliner Staatsoper in der Spielzeit 1937/38 unter der Leitung von Wilhelm Furtwängler, einem ihrer wichtigsten Dirigenten: »Ich hatte nur den einen Gedanken, in dieser Aufführung gesanglich und darstellerisch den Eindruck einer unaufhörlichen Intuition zu übermitteln. Es ist schwer zu erklären, aus welchen Quellen ich schöpfte, aber das große Wunder gelang mir. Vielleicht war es das Fegefeuer, in dem ich mich menschlich befand, oder mein unerschöpfliches Talent, das die Natur mir verliehen hatte.« [5]

Bei den Bayreuther Festspielen ist Frida Leider ab 1928 ein gefragter Gast, zunächst als Kundry, in den Folgejahren auch als Isolde und Brünnhilde. Festspielchef Siegfried Wagner lässt ihr vor allem bei der szenischen Darstellung der Brünnhilden gestalterische Spielräume, die sie mittlerweile überzeugend nutzt. In ihren Anfangsjahren musste sie sich immer wieder Defizite in ihren schauspielerischen Leistungen nachsagen lassen, die sich damals weitgehend auf Posen reduzierten.

Als die Nationalsozialisten 1933 an die Macht kommen, steht Frida Leider im Zenit ihrer Laufbahn, doch fällt es ihr zunehmend schwerer, die schrecklichen politischen Ereignisse zu verdrängen. Ihr jüdischer Mann emigriert noch rechtzeitig in die Schweiz, sie selbst darf ab 1938 kaum noch im Ausland gastieren. Nach Ausbruch des Zweiten Weltkriegs muss sie ihre künstlerische Tätigkeit auch in Deutschland reduzieren und schließlich ganz aufgeben. Die Folgen sind eine schwere Depression und ein gesundheitlicher Zusammenbruch.

Nach Kriegsende kehren ihre Lebensgeister noch einmal zurück, doch tritt Frida Leider nur noch vereinzelt als Liedinterpretin auf. Nach ihrem Bühnenabschied kehrt sie als Regisseurin an die Berliner Staatsoper zurück und eröffnet ein Opernstudio für junge Sänger.

Geblieben sind nach ihrem Tod im Juni 1975 zahlreiche Plattenaufnahmen, die Frida Leider bis heute als eine der Größten ihres Faches ausweisen. Dabei war ihr Wagner-Verständnis keineswegs auf ein großes, imposantes Volumen ausgerichtet. Vielmehr bewahrte sie fest in ihrem Herzen, was Richard Wagner selbst den Sängern mit auf den Weg gab. Im Durchgang zur Festspielbühne in Bayreuth, erinnert sich die Sopranistin, steht eine Mahnung des Komponisten zu lesen: »Achtung auf die kleinen Noten; die großen kommen von selbst!« 6

Frida Leider als Brünnhilde, Bayreuth 1927

Frida Leider als Isolde, Staatsoper Berlin, ca. 1937

Frida Leider, *18th April 1888 in Berlin

Winged helmets, real horses, and blazing pyres: the era of the 1920s and 30s, in which Frida Leider rises to become one of the greatest Wagnerian heroines, is characterised by grand, realistic stagings that in the New Bayreuth of Wieland Wagner already seem inconceivable. The Brünnhildes still wear leaden armour at the *Todesverkündigung* (*Annunciation of Death*, Act II): »Helmet and armor, shield and spear could hardly be raised«, Frida Leider writes in her memoirs. »In the truest sense of the word I sang: *Schwer wiegt mir der Waffen Wucht* (*My load of armour weighs heavy on me*).« [1]

Above all, the very naturalistic staging of *Götterdämmerung* at the Waldoper Zoppot poses an additional theatrical trial for the soprano: »Grane (Brünnhilde's horse) just loved to nibble on my wig while scratching with its hoof, which of course meant a request for sugar, but heaven knows I was busy with other things and glad when the horse was fairly quiet. [...] While the funeral pyre was ablaze there was a policeman in Brünnhilde's costume and wig in the backdrop of foliage who jumped on a horse and made a daring leap over the burning pyre.« [2]

Frida Leider is often rightly acknowledged as the pinnacle of highly dramatic Wagnerian specialists. Even in the highest vocal peaks this soprano shines with power and majesty. Without the slightest breaks between registers, her voice is always dark, clear and beautiful. The critics agree: »What a sure and lofty sound she produces, and how lyrically she shapes her tones«, raves the *Wiener Zeitung* in 1932.

The soprano sings her Wagnerian roles in the *bel canto* style: »I studied very closely Wagner's dynamic instructions and gradually came to the realization that my vocal technique and Richard Wagner's demands would certainly bring about an artistic result.« [3]

Frida's talent attracts attention early on in school but vocal studies are prevented by a lack of money. In an era in which women slowly but tenaciously blaze a trail into men's trades, Frida Leider is one of the first to enter a commercial profession. She takes private singing lessons on the side.

The decisive turning point comes when she auditions for the chorus of the Royal Opera House in Berlin just before the outbreak of the First World War. The conductor recognizes her dramatic potential and urges her to get trained as a soloist. Her mother takes on an office job so that Frida can fully concentrate on singing.

Her first engagements lead the soprano to the relatively small stages of Halle, Rostock and Königsberg. In 1919 she comes to Hamburg, her first big house. When in 1923 the long-cherished dream of a firm engagement is fulfilled at the Berliner Staatsoper, Frida Leider is 35 years old, technically prepared to dazzle, a strong, seasoned player now ready for an inter-national career.

Time and again it is Isolde who brings her luck in the crucial moments. Already in the early 1920s the Hamburg Opera's general manager Löwenfeld predicts elatedly that he will make her the greatest Isolde of all time. She later makes her debut in this role in London and at New York's Metropolitan Opera, where she scores great triumphs.

Leider's fondest memory is a *Tristan* performance at the Berliner Staatsoper during the 1937/38 season under the baton of Wilhelm Furtwängler, one of her most important conduc-tors: »I had only one thought: to vocally and dramatically convey the impression of constant intuition. It is difficult to explain from which sources I drew, but somehow I managed that great miracle. Maybe it was the very human purgatory in which I found myself or the inexhaustible talent that nature had granted me.« [4]

Frida Leider is, of course, also in demand as a guest performer at the Bayreuth Festival. Under the artistic direction of Siegfried Wagner she makes her debut as Kundry in 1928; in subsequent years she also appears as Isolde and Brünnhilde. Above all, for the theatrical portrayal of Brünnhilde the festival manager gives her creative freedom which she now employs in a convincing way. In her early years she had repeatedly been criticised for deficiencies in her acting, which was largely reduced to a series of poses.

When the Nazis come to power in 1933, Frida Leider is at the zenith of her career but she finds it increasingly difficult to repress the terrible political events.

In the nick of time her Jewish husband emigrates to Switzerland, but from 1938 on she is only rarely permitted to make guest appearances abroad. After the outbreak of World War II she has to reduce her artistic activity in Germany and eventually give it up altogether. She consequently suffers a breakdown and severe depression.

When her spirits return after the war, Frida Leider reappears, alas only sporadically, as a lieder singer. After her farewell to the stage she returns to the Berliner Staatsoper as a director and opens an opera studio for young singers.

What remains after her death in June 1975 are numerous recordings that identify Frida Leider as one of the greatest in her field to this day. Her understanding of Wagner was not focused on great impressive volume. Instead, she kept firmly in her heart what Richard Wagner himself had given singers to equip them on their way. As Frida Leider remembers, there is a written reminder by the composer in the passageway to the festival stage at Bayreuth: »Mind the small notes; the big ones take care of themselves!« [5]

Kirsten Flagstad, *12. Juli 1895 in Hamar, Norwegen

Mit wenigen Worten formuliert sie die vielleicht schönste Liebeserklärung einer Interpretin an einen Komponisten: »Wagner hat mich ganz und gar erfüllt«, oder besser noch im englischen Original: »Wagner was sufficient for me.« [1]

Dabei ist Kirsten Flagstad mitnichten eine einseitige Künstlerin. Ihr reiches Repertoire umfasst über 50 Rollen in Werken vom Hochbarock bis zur Spätromantik. Der Schöpfer des *Tristans* aber fasziniert sie unter allen am meisten.

182 Male (!) und damit »mehr als genug für ein ganzes Leben«, wie die Norwegerin selbst in ihren Memoiren bilanziert, steht sie als Isolde auf der Bühne, darunter allein 48 Male an der berühmten New Yorker Met an der Seite ihres ebenbürtigen Bühnenpartners Lauritz Melchior. In einem viel zitierten Interview resümiert der damalige Intendant dieses Hauses, Giulio Gatti-Casazza stolz, Caruso und Flagstad seien seine größten Entdeckungen, die ihm diese Bühne verdanke. [2]

Solche Superlative erscheinen auch aus heutiger Sicht nicht übertrieben, bestätigen doch zahlreiche Tondokumente Flagstads musikalische Meisterschaft.

Als legendär gilt vor allem die späte *Tristan*-Aufnahme unter Wilhelm Furtwängler aus dem Jahr 1952. Im fortgeschrittenen Alter von 57 Jahren hat die monumentale, majestätische Stimme nichts von ihrer betörenden Schönheit und Klangfülle verloren. Plattengeschichte geschrieben hat diese Aufnahme freilich auch deshalb, weil Elisabeth Schwarzkopf einige Spitzentöne für die Kollegin übernommen hat, aber das hört allenfalls, wer darum weiß und mindert nicht die großartige Gesamtleistung Flagstads. Gelungen ist hier vielmehr dank dem unmerklichen Verschmelzen der Stimmen zweier Jahrhundertsängerinnen ein genialer Coup. Als letzte Zeitzeugin erinnerte sich Elisabeth Furtwängler gern daran, wie dicht Schwarzkopf im Studio auf einem Stuhl direkt hinter der Kollegin stand, auf dass die Übergänge organisch gelingen mögen.

Kaum vorstellbar, dass Kirsten Flagstad um ein Haar das Singen gar nicht zu ihrem Beruf gemacht hätte. Und das, obwohl sich ihr künstlerisches Talent im frühen Kindesalter ankündigt, und sie schon als Zehnjährige den *Lohengrin* studiert.

Mit 18 debütiert Kirsten in Oslo als Nuri in D'Alberts *Tiefland*, Studien in Stockholm schließen sich an. Im Laufe der kommenden Jahre erarbeitet sie sich zahlreiche anspruchsvolle Partien von Mozart, Verdi und Puccini, und so schnell, wie die junge Sängerin sie alle beherrscht, wundert es kaum, dass Alexander Varnay, Vater von Astrid Varnay und Leiter der *Opéra Comique* in Oslo, schon bald über sie ins Schwärmen gerät: »Kirsten kann alles – Kirsten can do anything.«

Als die junge Frau aber nach der Trennung von ihrem ersten Mann 1930 den vermögenden Industriellen und Großhändler Henry Johansen in zweiter Ehe heiratet, erwägt sie überraschend, ihren Beruf aufzugeben: »Ich musste ja mein eigenes Geld nicht mehr verdienen, und das Singen bedeutet harte Arbeit.« [3]

Die skandinavische Musikwelt aber will nicht auf sie verzichten und überhäuft sie mit Anfragen. Flagstad kann den attraktiven Angeboten nicht widerstehen, verwirft ihren Plan von einem geruhsamen Hausfrauen-Dasein und nimmt das Singen wieder auf.

Ihr Weg führt über Göteborg und Oslo recht zügig an die New Yorker Met, an der sie die Nachfolge für die eben abgetretene Frida Leider antritt und schon mit ihrem Debüt als Sieglinde für Furore sorgt. Die enorme Resonanz auf diese vom Rundfunk übertragene Aufführung der *Walküre* übertrifft alle Erwartungen. Für die amerikanische Musikwelt ist die in diesem Land bis dahin noch völlig Unbekannte eine große Entdeckung und bald auch schon ein Kassenmagnet.

Nur wenige Tage liegen zwischen diesem sensationellen Durchbruch und Flagstads erstem, ebenfalls hymnisch gefeierten *Tristan* an diesem Haus. »Transzendental schön« [4] ist ihre Isolde und erinnert daran, dass Wagners Partitur »keine Hausfrau mit roter Perücke« vorsieht, wie man sie zuvor oft gesehen hat, sondern »eine irische Maid.« [5]

Ihren großen Erfolg hat sie sich indes schwer verdient. Die ersten Monate in der neuen Wahlheimat gestalten sich ungemein arbeitsintensiv, gönnt der Intendant ihr doch nur wenige Ruhepausen. Eine Premiere jagt die nächste. Ausgerechnet als ihre erste Brünnhilde in der *Walküre* ansteht, plagt Kirsten Flagstad zudem eine schwere Grippe, der zufolge sie viele Proben absagen muss. Trotz solch widriger Umstände meistert die eisern disziplinierte, willensstarke Nordin ihren Part mit Bravour, wie einmal mehr dem emphatischen Presse-Echo zu entnehmen. – Flagstads »göttliche Erhabenheit« in der *Todesverkündigung* heben einige Kritiker ganz besonders hervor.

Dass die Heroine ihr Publikum schließlich noch einmal ganz besonders stark in der *Götterdämmerung* bewegt haben muss, dokumentiert eine Kritik in der *Times*. Darin heißt es, kein Zuschauer werde vergessen, wie zärtlich sie in ihrem Schlussgesang dem gefallenen Helden huldigt, mit majestätischer Geste befiehlt, einen Scheiterhaufen zu errichten, und entschlossen bis zum unausweichlichen Ende ihrer Bestimmung folgt.

Noch viele solche großen Triumphe feiert Kirsten Flagstad an der Met, bis sie 1941 ein starkes Heimweh und große Sehnsucht nach ihrem geliebten Mann überwältigt. Sie scheut keine Mühen, über etliche Umwege in das von den Deutschen besetzte Norwegen zurückzukehren. Nach dem Krieg ist dies einer der Gründe dafür, warum der Sopranistin zu Unrecht Kooperation mit den Nazis unterstellt wird.

Noch nicht einmal die Aufführungsgeschichte der Bayreuther Festspiele in ihrer dunkelsten Ära der NS-Zeit hat Kirsten Flagstad entscheidend mitgeschrieben. Nach ihren ersten Auftritten auf dem Grünen Hügel im Sommer 1933 in kleineren Rollen ist sie nur ein Jahr später noch einmal als Gutrune und Sieglinde an diesen Ort zurückgekehrt.

Glücklicherweise aber kann sich Kirsten Flagstad »auf die Stimmbänder verlassen wie ein Athlet auf seine Muskeln«, wie Jürgen Kesting in seinem Sängerlexikon kommentiert, und so bewährt sich die einstige Amazone auf der Bühne nun als eine ebensolche im wirklichen Leben. Die Schlagzeilen in der Presse ignoriert sie, an Menschen, die sich zum Protest gegen sie vor den Konzertsälen versammeln, zieht sie stolz erhobenen Hauptes vorbei und verzaubert hernach mit ihrem wunderbaren Gesang das Publikum im Saal.

Überwiegend in England und in den USA setzt sie ihre Karriere nach dem Krieg fort, macht sich etwa auch unsterblich als Interpretin der Uraufführung von Richard Strauss' *Vier Letzten Liedern* unter Wilhelm Furtwängler.

Nach ihrem Rückzug von der Bühne wird Kirsten Flagstad Intendantin der Oper in Oslo. Am 7. Dezember 1962 stirbt mit ihr eine der bedeutendsten Wagnerinterpretinnen aller Zeiten.

Kirsten Flagstad als Brünnhilde,
Metropolitan Opera New York 1935

Kirsten Flagstad als Isolde, Rollendebüt an der
Metropolitan Opera New York, 6. Februar 1935

Kirsten Flagstad, *12th July 1895 in Hamar, Norway

In a few words she utters possibly the most beautiful declaration of love by a performer for a composer: »Wagner was sufficient for me.« [1]

Kirsten Flagstad is, to be sure, no one-dimensional artist. Her rich repertoire includes over fifty roles in operas from the High Baroque to the Late Romantic era. But it is the creator of *Tristan* who fascinates her most of all.

She performed Isolde 182 times – »enough Isoldes for a lifetime!«, the Norwegian soprano notes in her memoirs. These include the 48 times she sang it at New York's pre-eminent Met alongside her ideally paired co-star Lauritz Melchior. In an oft-quoted interview the general manager at that time, Giulio Gatti-Casazza, proudly concludes that the discovery of Caruso and Flagstad represents his greatest contribution to the stage. [2]

Even from today's perspective such superlatives seem no exaggeration, for countless recordings confirm Flagstad's musical achievement.

Towering over all are the late and legendary *Tristan* recordings of 1952 under Wilhelm Furtwängler. At the ripe age of fifty-seven her monumental, majestic voice had lost none of its ravishing beauty and sonority. This *Tristan* also made recording history when Elisabeth Schwarzkopf dubbed some top notes for her colleague. Yet this is audible only to those who know about it, and in no way does it diminish the greatness of Flagstad's overall performance. Instead it represents a brilliant coup in the blending of voices from two legendary performers of the century. Elisabeth Furtwängler, the last contemporary witness, recalled how Schwarzkopf stood on a chair right behind Flagstad in the studio so that the vocal transitions would be as smooth as possible.

It is hard to imagine that Kirsten Flagstad almost, by a hair's breadth, chose not to make singing her profession – despite the fact that her artistic talent already was evident in early childhood: as a ten-year-old, she could be found studying the score of *Lohengrin*.

At the age of eighteen Kirsten debuts in Oslo as Nuri in D'Alberts *Tiefland*. Musical studies in Stockholm soon follow. In the ensuing years she works on a range of demanding roles by Mozart, Verdi and Puccini. The young singer masters them all so quickly that soon enough – and not surprisingly – Alexander Varnay, Astrid Varnay's father and the director of the Opéra Comique in Oslo, goes into rhapsodies over her: »Kirsten can do anything.«

Then in 1930, following a divorce from her first husband, the young singer marries the industrialist and wholesaler Henry Johansen, and surprisingly considers abandoning her career: »I didn't have to earn my own money any more and I thought it was time to give it up [...] It had been hard, unrelenting work.« [3]

However, the Scandinavian music world does not want to relinquish her and overwhelms her with requests. Flagstad cannot resist these attractive invitations: she jettisons her plan to become a wife of leisure, and she resumes singing.

Her path from Göteborg and Oslo soon leads to New York's Metropolitan Opera, where she succeeds the recently cast Frida Leider and makes a sensational debut as Sieglinde. The huge response to this performance of *Die Walküre*, which is broadcast over the radio, exceeds all expectations. To the American music world, to which she has been heretofore entirely unknown, Flagstad is a great discovery and soon becomes a major box-office draw.

Just a few days pass between this sensational breakthrough and Flagstad's first and equally celebrated performance in *Tristan* at the Met. Her Isolde is »transcendentally beautiful« [4] and reminds us that there is no basis in Wagner's libretto or music for Isolde to be represented as a »Hausfrau in a red wig«, as one so often sees on stage, but rather an »Irish Maiden.« [5]

But great success is hard earned. The first months in her new adopted country are rather grueling since the Met's general manager grants her hardly any breathing space as one debut follows the next. Just before her debut as Brünnhilde in *Die Walküre*, she comes down with a severe case of flu and is forced to cancel a series of rehearsals. Yet in the face of such adversity the disciplined and determined Norwegian masters her part with flying colors, as reflected once again in rave reviews: Flagstad's »Olympian serenity« in the *Todesverkündigung* (*Annunciation of Death*) is highlighted by several critics.

The extent to which the heroine ultimately moved her audience again in *Götterdämmerung* (*Twilight of the Gods*) is recorded by the reviewer in the *Times*: »No one who saw it will forget that entrance, the apostrophe to what had been and was to be; the tender homage to the fallen hero; the majesty of the gesture that commanded the preparation of the funeral pyre; the realisation by her to whom at last everything was revealed of the inevitable end, and the cleansing atonement that it was her destiny to proffer.«

Kirsten Flagstad celebrates so many other great triumphs at the Met until, in 1941, she becomes so homesick for her beloved husband that she spares no effort to get back, through several detours, to Norway, now under German occupation. This is one of the reasons why after the war she is unjustly alleged to have cooperated with the Nazis.

In fact she never even played a leading role at the Bayreuth Festival during its darkest days of the Nazi era. After her first performances on the Green Hill in minor parts in the summer of 1933, she returned only once the next year to sing Gutrune and Sieglinde.

Fortunately, Kirsten Flagstad can »rely on her vocal chords like an athlete on his or her muscles«, Jürgen Kesting comments in his book of great singers. The former Amazon on stage now proves to be no less formidable in life. Ignoring the newspaper headlines, with her head held high she passes by the people gathered in protest outside the concert halls, and then enchants the audience inside with her glorious singing.

It is mainly in Great Britain and the United States that she pursues her career after the war, and then immortalizes herself as a performer in the premiere of Richard Strauss' *Vier Letzte Lieder* (*Four Last Songs*) under Wilhelm Furtwängler.

In her last years, after her retirement from the stage, Kirsten Flagstad serves as general manager of the Oslo Opera. Her death on 7 December 1962 in Oslo marks the passing of one of the greatest Wagnerian singers of all time.

Martha Mödl. * 22. März 1912 in Nürnberg

Als einen »Zauberkasten« bezeichnet sie Wilhelm Furtwängler treffend, weil sich ihre Stimme stets mit ihren Bühnenfiguren verwandelt. Es sind diese absolute Identifikation mit ihrer Rolle und die untrennbare Einheit von Gesang, Persönlichkeit und Darstellung, die Martha Mödl groß macht und die auch Wieland Wagner fasziniert, der sie in dieser Hinsicht mit Wilhelmine Schröder-Devrient vergleicht, der Lieblingsinterpretin seines Großvaters.

Schon 1951, zur Eröffnung der ersten Festspiele auf dem Grünen Hügel nach Kriegsende, wird die gebürtige Nürnbergerin als Kundry im *Parsifal* zur Idealbesetzung des Neu-Bayreuther Festspielchefs. Es ist der Auftakt zu der einmaligen, knapp 60 Jahre während Karriere einer Ausnahmesängerin, die sich die größten und schwierigsten Wagner-Partien stupend mehr oder minder im Selbststudium erarbeitet, entscheidend gestützt durch ihren Instinkt, ihre Intuition und eine einmalige Naturstimme.

Martha Mödls musikalisches Talent fällt schon früh in der Schule auf, doch ist in den wirtschaftlich schwierigen 1930er Jahren an ein Gesangsstudium nicht zu denken, erst recht nicht, als auch noch der Vater die Familie verlässt. Als Buchhalterin muss sie für ihren Lebensunterhalt hart arbeiten und mehrfach umziehen. Als sie endlich Gesangsunterricht nehmen kann, ist sie bereits 28 Jahre alt. Mittlerweile ist der Krieg ausgebrochen, der Studentin bleibt kaum mehr Zeit, als die Anfangsgründe des Singens zu erlernen. Immerhin gelingt trotz dieser ungünstigen Voraussetzungen ein schneller Einstieg in die Sängerlaufbahn, zunächst als Mezzosopran.

Einige Jahre nach Kriegsende wechselt die Autodidaktin ihr Fach, prägt auf dem Grünen Hügel als Hochdramatische der ersten Stunde den abstrakt-statuarischen Regiestil des »Entrümplers« Wieland Wagner mit und wird – so wie sie ihren Partien psychologisch tief auf den Grund geht – für zwei Jahrzehnte zu einer Bayreuther Institution. Eine Perfektionistin freilich ist sie nicht, aber das strebt sie auch nicht an. Nie denkt sie auch nur eine Minute an technische Dinge, wenn sie auf der Bühne steht, auch auf die Gefahr hin, dass mitunter ein hoher Ton verrutscht. Es ist vielmehr ihre Hingabe an die Musik, die Martha Mödl in besonderer Weise auszeichnet, sich in ihrer ganzen Persönlichkeit ausdrückt. Bezeichnenderweise verzichtet sie auf ein Privatleben, auf Ehe und Familie, und widmet ihre ganze Kraft allein dem Theater.

Nicht zufällig wird Martha Mödl mehrfach mit Maria Callas verglichen, besticht sie doch wie sie auf der Bühne als eine große Tragödin. Die Isolde wird bald zu einer der Figuren, mit denen sie Maßstäbe setzt: »Ihre dramatische Agilität im ersten, ihre lyrisch-keusche Verhaltenheit im zweiten, ihren steinernen Schmerz im letzten Bild wird keiner je vergessen«, heißt es in einer Kritik der *Süddeutschen Zeitung* vom Juli 1952 zu ihrer Isolde in Bayreuth unter Herbert von Karajan. Wieland Wagner hebt die »unheimliche, dämonische Besessenheit in dem *Frau Minne kenntest du nicht?*« [1] hervor. Der Berliner Komponist Aribert Reimann, der die Heroine als Isolde an der Städtischen Oper Berlin erlebte, erinnert sich in seinem Nachruf besonders an den *Liebestod*. Ihm sind »der hell gefärbte, fast ätherisch gewordene Klang ihrer Stimme, das sanfte Entschweben, das scheinbare Heraustreten aus ihrem Körper, die anrührende Gestik« unvergesslich geblieben. [2]

So enorm sich Mödls Stimme in den oberen Registern entwickelt, bleiben ihre Mezzo-Wurzeln angesichts des dunklen Timbres unverkennbar. Wieland Wagners Vorstellungen kommt das sehr entgegen, er erkennt die erotische Faszination, die von dieser erdigen Grundfärbung ausgeht, und auch die Interpretin selbst bekräftigt Jahrzehnte später, dass diese Partie doch vor allem eine gute Mittellage erfordere: »Heute singt jede Sopranistin, die blendend hohe Töne hat, die Isolde, und das ist falsch«, [3] sagt Martha Mödl 1984 in einem Interview; eine dunkle Stimme harmoniere viel treffender mit dem Charakter und den Lebenserfahrungen dieser Figur.

Nach ihren eigenen Worten ist ihre Lieblingsrolle aber die Brünnhilde, vor allem in der *Götterdämmerung*. Hier besticht Martha Mödl abermals als große Tragödin. Die »ungeheure Gefühlsskala vom Heroischen zur Zerknirschung, vom Liebespathos zum Hass« sei nie so durchlaufen worden wie von dieser Brünnhilde, schreibt treffend der Musikkritiker Hans Heinz Stuckenschmidt. [4]

Wieland Wagner beeindruckt vor allem ihr *Welch banger Träume Mären*, hatte sie doch »nach der großen Stunde der Altistin in der Waltrautenerzählung als Brünnhilde immer die Tiefe, die der Kollegin fehlte«. [5]

Legendär ist die *Ring*-Gesamtaufnahme unter Wilhelm Furtwängler, aufgenommen 1953 in Rom mit dem Sinfonieorchester des italienischen Rundfunks. Besondere Beachtung in dieser Edition verdient Brünnhildes Schlussgesang in der *Götterdämmerung*. »Ruhe, ruhe du Gott« heißt es darin zum Ende hin. Worte, die bei Martha Mödl wie bei keiner anderen erfüllt sind von Trauer, Schwere, einem heiligen Ernst, auch von einem inneren Frieden. Dieses reiche Ausdrucksspektrum rührt auch Astrid Varnay stark an, die in ihrem persönlichen Nachruf auf die ebenbürtige Kollegin bekennt: »Martha traf einen damit ins Herz.« [6]

Wer sich derart mit Haut und Haaren seiner Existenz als Sängerschauspieler verschreibt, kann sich freilich mit dem Gedanken an einen Abschied von der Bühne schwer anfreunden. Im Gegensatz zu manchen anderen Kolleginnen, die im fortgeschrittenen Alter an Partien festhalten, denen sie nicht mehr gewachsen sind, ist Martha Mödl so weise, wieder in ihr ursprüngliches Mezzofach zurückzukehren. Sie spezialisiert sich auf Charakterrollen von Richard Strauss (Klytämnestra, Herodias, Die Amme in *Die Frau ohne Schatten*), Janáček (Die Küsterin in *Jenůfa*), Tschaikowski (Die Gräfin in *Pique Dame*), Mussorgski (Die Amme in *Boris Godunow*) und Weill (Leokadja Begbick in *Aufstieg und Fall der Stadt Mahagonny*), die sie mit ebensolchem Furor meistert wie zuvor ihre Wagnerheldinnen. – Unvergessen sind auch ihre Auftritte in zeitgenössischen Werken von Hans Werner Henze (*Elegie für junge Liebende*), Wolfgang Fortner (*Bluthochzeit, Elisabeth Tudor*) oder Aribert Reimann, der ihr seine *Melusine* und seine *Gespenstersonate* widmet.

Mit ihrem Tod am 17. Dezember 2001 endet eine große Ära der Darstellungskunst. Nur wenige Hochdramatische haben vergleichbar nachhaltig Aufführungsgeschichte geschrieben. Wie bemerkte doch Wieland Wagner so treffend: »Kundry! Isolde! Brünnhilde! Keine wie du!«

Martha Mödl als Kundry, Debüt zur
Eröffnung der Bayreuther Festspiele 1951

Martha Mödl als Isolde,
Theater an der Wien, 12.06.1954

Martha Mödl, * 22nd March 1912 in Nuremberg

Wilhelm Furtwängler aptly describes her as a »magic chest« since her voice keeps changing with her stage characters. It is this absolute identification with her role as well as the indivisible unity of voice, personality and presentation that makes Martha Mödl great. It also fascinates Wieland Wagner, who compares her in this respect to Wilhelmine Schröder-Devrient, his grandfather's favourite soprano.

As early as 1951, at the opening of the first Festival on the Green Hill after the war, the native from Nuremberg proves to the New Bayreuth Festival director to be the ideal casting as Kundry in *Parsifal*: It is the prelude to the unique, almost 60-year career of an exceptional singer who masters the greatest and most challenging Wagnerian roles astoundingly more or less through self-study, supported decisively by her instinct, her intuition and a unique natural voice.

Martha Mödl's musical talent attracts attention early on in school but during the dire economic conditions of the Thirties formal vocal studies are out of the question, especially after her father has left the family. She has to work hard for her living as an accountant and has to relocate often. By the time she can finally take singing lessons, she is already 28 years old. Meanwhile, war has broken out and the student has time for little more than to learn the rudiments of singing. Nevertheless, despite these unfavourable conditions she soon manages to jump-start a singing career, first as a mezzo-soprano.

Several years after the war the self-taught soprano takes on new roles and provides the first hour of high drama at the Festspiele as she embodies the »new broom« Wieland Wagner's abstract and statuesque style of directing. Distinguished by her ability to plumb the psychological depths of her roles, she becomes a Bayreuth institution for two decades. To be sure, she is no perfectionist, nor does she seek to be one. She never thinks of technical points when on stage, even at the risk of occasionally missing a high note. Rather, it is her dedication to the music that characterizes Martha Mödl in a special way. Significantly, she for-goes a private life – no husband, no family – devoting all her energies to the theatre alone.

It is no coincidence that Martha Mödl is repeatedly compared with Maria Callas, dominating the stage as a great tragedienne just like *La Divina*.

Isolde soon becomes one of the roles with which Mödl sets new standards. »Her dramatic agility in the first, her lyrical and chaste restraint in the second, her stony pain in the last tableau no one will ever forget«, as a review in the *Süddeutsche Zeitung* in July 1952 describes her Isolde in Bayreuth under Herbert von Karajan. Wieland Wagner emphasizes the »unearthly demonic possession in *Frau Minne kenntest du nicht?*« [1] In his obituary, the Berlin composer Aribert Reimann, who experienced the heroine at the Städtische Oper Berlin, stresses her *Liebestod*. To him, »the light-coloured, almost ethereal sound of her voice, the soft wafting, its apparent emergence from her body, the touching gestures« remain unforgettable. [2]

Mödl's voice develops enormously in the upper registers, but her dark timbre unmistakably reveals her roots as a mezzo. Wieland Wagner finds this quality most appealing, as he recognizes the erotic fascination of this earthy ground colour. Decades later Mödl herself asserts that, above all, the part requires a good central position: »Today, every soprano with dazzling high notes sings Isolde, but that's wrong«, [3] Mödl observes in a 1984 interview, since a darker timbre is better suited to Isolde's character and experiences.

But in her own words her favourite character is Brünnhilde, especially in *Götterdämmerung (Twilight of the Gods)*. Here again Martha Mödl is utterly captivating as a great tragedienne. The »immense scale of emotional expression – from the heroic to contrition, from the pathos of love to hate« has never been so traversed as by this Brünnhilde, as the music critic Hans Heinz Stuckenschmidt aptly notes. [4]

Wieland Wagner is particularly impressed by her *Welch banger Träume Mären (What tales of tortured dreams)* because »after the great hour of the alto in Waltraute's narrative, as Brünnhilde Mödl always had the depth that her colleague lacked.« [5]

The complete *Ring* Cycle under Wilhelm Furtwängler, recorded in Rome in 1953 with the Italian Radio Symphony Orchestra, is legendary. In this recording Brünnhilde's final scene in *Götterdämmerung* deserves special attention. *Ruhe, ruhe du Gott (Peace, peace, you God)* she sings toward the end. Words that Martha Mödl, like no other singer, fills with sorrow, gravity, a holy solemnity, but also an inner peace. This rich range of expression deeply touches Astrid Varnay as well, who confesses in a personal tribute to her colleague and peer: »Martha struck your heart with it.« [6]

Yet unlike so many colleagues who cling to their old roles long past their ability to master them, Marta Mödl wisely decides to return to her initial career as a mezzo. She specialises in character roles by Richard Strauss (Clytemnestra, Herodias, The Nurse in *Die Frau ohne Schatten*), Janáček (Kostelnička, *the Sextoness* in *Jenůfa*), Tchaikovsky (The Countess in *Pique Dame*) and Weill (Leocadia Begbick in *Rise and Fall of the City of Mahagonny*), which she finesses as dramatically as her Wagnerian heroines of yesterday. Also memorable are her roles in contemporary works by Hans Werner Henze (*Elegy for Young Lovers*),

Wolfgang Fortner (*Blood Wedding, Elizabeth Tudor*) and Aribert Reimann, who dedicates his *Melusine* and his *Ghost Sonata* to her.

Her death on 17 December 2001 marked the end of a great era of opera stars. Only a few highly dramatic singers have made such lasting stage history. As Wieland Wagner observed so fittingly: »Kundry! Isolde! Brünnhilde! There's no one like you!«

Astrid Varnay, *25. April 1918 in Stockholm

Ihre Vorliebe gilt den dunklen Seiten des menschlichen Charakters, finsteren, abgründigen Gestalten. Eine Favoritin unter ihren Wagnerfiguren ist folgerichtig die listige, intrigante Ortrud (*Lohengrin*). In ihren Memoiren berichtet Astrid Varnay, dass die Kinder des Bayreuther Festspielchefs Wolfgang Wagner regelrecht Angst hatten, sich hinter der Bühne in ihre Nähe zu begeben, weil sie in dieser Rolle so streng wirkte.

Doch nutzt Ortrud ihre scharfe Intelligenz auch, um ihr Schicksal in die eigene Hand zu nehmen, im Gegensatz zu Elsa ist sie auf keinen Retter angewiesen. Allein dieser Unabhängigkeit wegen imponiert sie Varnay, die an den »Unschuldslämmern« Elsa und Elisabeth schon in jungen Jahren bald das Interesse verliert.

Astrid Varnay emanzipiert sich auch in ihrem eigenen Leben, lange vor der autonomen Frauenbewegung Ende der 1960er Jahre. Eine bürgerliche Existenz in der traditionellen Rolle als Hausfrau und Mutter kommt für sie nicht infrage. Ein Single soll sie gleichwohl nicht bleiben. Der ideale Ehepartner scheint wie von einer höheren Macht für sie bestimmt zu sein: Hermann Weigert, begabter Opernpädagoge und Chefkorrepetitor der Metropolitan Opera. 1939 nimmt er Astrid zunächst als Mentor unter seine Fittiche, 1945 wird der deutsch-jüdische Emigrant auch ihr Partner fürs Leben.

Kirsten Flagstad, eine gute Freundin der Familie, ist gewissermaßen eine Patin dieser kinderlosen, harmonischen Verbindung. Sie stellt in Varnays Laufbahn entscheidende Weichen mit ihren Empfehlungen an Weigert und an die Bayreuther Festspiele. In den Biografien der Kolleginnen gibt es auffällige Parallelen: Beide wachsen in einer Künstlerfamilie auf, werden im Singen von ihren Müttern unterwiesen und beginnen ihre Bühnenlaufbahn schon in sehr jungem Alter, beide verschlägt es für viele Jahre von Skandinavien nach Amerika.

Oft kreuzen sich die Wege der Heroinen auf denkwürdige Weise, zweimal begegnen sie sich 1951 als Partnerinnen in der *Walküre*: Bei einer Radio-Matinee an der Met ist Varnay die Sieglinde und Flagstad die Brünnhilde, wenige Monate später bei Flagstads historischem Abschied als Wagnersängerin in Covent Garden am 31. Mai tauschen sie die Rollen; letztere Aufführung ist für beide eine ganz besondere. Sehr anrührend beschreibt Varnay in ihren Lebenserinnerungen, wie bescheiden die Norwegerin ihr beim Schlussbeifall plötzlich das Feld überließ: »Auf einmal war sie nicht mehr an meiner Seite, ließ mich auf dem Platz stehen, den sie soeben geräumt hatte [...]. Auf wunderbar symbolische Weise schien sie mir sagen zu wollen: ›Übernimm du‹. Für mich war dieser heilige Auftrag einer großherzigen Frau wie ein Ritterschlag.«[1]

Schon in Astrids frühester Kindheit geht es turbulent zu. Ihre ungarischen Eltern reisen mit dem Mädchen um die halbe Welt, kaum dass sie sechs Jahre alt ist – von Skandinavien über Süd- nach Nordamerika. Als die Familie in New York ankommt, stirbt schon bald der Vater und Astrid muss einen Beruf ergreifen, um zum Lebensunterhalt beizutragen. Sie arbeitet zunächst als Sekretärin, den Gesangsunterricht bei Weigert verdient sie sich mit einem Nebenjob in einer Buchhandlung.

Nie im Leben aber hätte es sich die junge Frau träumen lassen, dass ihr erstes Engagement sie an die Met führen würde. Zu der Zeit heißt sie mit erstem Vornamen noch Violet, doch legt sie diesen ihrem Agenten zuliebe schnell ab.

Knapp 23 Jahre alt ist Astrid, als sich ihr eine einmalige Chance bietet: Die berühmte Lotte Lehmann erkrankt kurzfristig, Varnay übernimmt für sie die Sieglinde in einer vom Radio live mitgeschnittenen Aufführung der *Walküre*. Wir schreiben den 6. Dezember 1941.

Mit ihrem souveränen Auftreten übertrifft die Debütantin jegliche Erwartungen, über Nacht ist sie in aller Munde. Doch damit nicht genug: Sechs Tage später erkrankt die stimmgewaltige Amerikanerin Helen Traubel, und Varnay muss für sie die Brünnhilde übernehmen. Die junge Interpretin kommt sich vor »wie Aschenbrödel, das plötzlich einen silbernen Schuh trägt und vom Prinzen erlöst wird.«[2]

Fortan bestreitet sie erfolgreich alle großen Wagnerpartien an der Met, und ausgerechnet ihr Debüt als Isolde gestaltet sich 1945 abermals recht nervenaufreibend: Wieder springt sie für Helen Traubel ein, diesmal allerdings mit besonders großem Lampenfieber, da sie einige Teile dieser Partie auf die Schnelle erst noch einstudieren musste.

Ihren ersten kompletten *Ring*-Zyklus als Brünnhilde allerdings meistert die Kosmopolitin erstmals 1948 in Buenos Aires.

Anfang der 1950er Jahre übersiedelt Astrid Varnay mit ihrem Ehemann nach Europa. Ihre künstlerische Heimat findet sie nun vor allem bei den Bayreuther Festspielen, wo sie von 1951 bis 1968 jährlich gastiert und wie Mödl und Nilsson eine feste Institution wird. Zu einer weiteren Stammbühne wird in späteren Jahren die Bayerische Staatsoper in München.

Im Gegensatz zu ihrer Freundin und Kollegin Mödl, die sich in ihren Partien mit der denkbar größten emotionalen Intensität verausgabt, will Varnay nicht die Kontrolle verlieren. »Schicht für Schicht« baut sie ihre Gestalten auf und zügelt ihre natürlichen Instinkte durch die »analytische Blaupause«.[3] So hört es sich auch an. Varnay und Mödl haben beide dunkle, kräftige Stimmen, aber Varnays Timbre wirkt etwas kühler und in der Tiefe weniger erdig. Im Gegenzug besitzt ihr Sopran in der Höhe stärkere Strahlkraft, und ihre schönsten Klänge sind ihre schwerelosen Kopftöne in den Spitzen.

Astrid Varnay ist ein Kopfmensch und als ein solcher ein eher seltenes Exemplar in der Opernwelt. Als Brünnhilde unterscheidet sie sich von ihren Kolleginnen besonders in der *Götterdämmerung*, wie sie scharfsichtig analysiert: Während die Nilsson hier stimmlich mit ihren »phänomenalen hohen Tönen« triumphiert und Mödl im Schlussgesang eine »Tiefe« erreicht wie keine andere, liege ihre Stärke »in der Intensität der dramatischen Szenen, besonders bei dem leidenschaftlichen Eid im zweiten Akt.« [4]

Mit ihrer Brünnhilde im *Ring* der ersten Bayreuther Festspiele nach Kriegsende entfacht Astrid Varnay auch im deutschen Feuilleton wahre Begeisterungsstürme. So bilanziert etwa der Kritiker der *Süddeutschen Zeitung*, ihre Brünnhilde sei sowohl hinsichtlich der »physischen als auch geistigen Bewältigung unübertroffen.« [5]

In den Folgejahren verfestigt sich dieses Bild: Varnay stelle »ein Phänomen an geistiger Durchdringung, stimmlicher Beherrschung und schauspielerischer Verwirklichung der Riesenpartie dar«, attestiert ihr abermals die *Süddeutsche Zeitung*. [6]

Zu ihren Paraderollen zählt fraglos auch die Isolde. Sie kommt Varnay in ihrem Wesen sehr entgegen, weil sie wie Ortrud in jeder Situation in der Lage ist, »die Initiative zu ergreifen, ohne Rücksicht darauf, wozu diese Entschlossenheit führen wird.« [7]

Es ist ein großes Versäumnis der Plattenindustrie, Varnays Wagnerinterpretationen nicht auf Tonträgern festzuhalten. Wie so manche andere Interpretinnen, etwa auch Ludmila Dvořáková, leidet Varnay hier unter der allzu großen Konkurrenz von Superstar Birgit Nilsson, nach der alle Labels hoffnungsvoll ihre Arme ausstrecken. Nilsson nimmt alle großen Wagneropern auf, danach sind die Budgets erschöpft. Die Labels übersehen, dass es für spätere Generationen einmal sehr interessant sein könnte, unterschiedliche erstklassige Interpretationen aus dieser Zeit zu vergleichen. Zumindest aber »Piraten« bringen zahlreiche wertvolle Live-Mitschnitte mit Astrid Varnay in Umlauf, sie sind mittlerweile auch legal zu erwerben.

Ende der 1960er Jahre endet die Wagnerkarriere der Nachkriegsheroine. Ihre letzten Brünnhilden verkörpert sie 1970 in Düsseldorf (*Walküre*) und Stuttgart (*Götterdämmerung*). Danach wechselt sie wie Martha Mödl ins Charakterfach, fasziniert ihr Publikum fortan als Klytämnestra (*Elektra*), Amme (*Die Frau ohne Schatten*), Herodias (*Salome*), Küsterin (*Jenůfa*), Leokadja Begbick (*Aufstieg und Fall der Stadt Mahagonny*) oder als Gräfin in *Pique Dame*.

Am 4. Dezember 2006 stirbt Astrid Varnay in München. Die Verfasser zahlreicher Nachrufe würdigen sie mit einem viel zitierten Ausruf Wieland Wagners, der ihr bodenständiges Wesen treffend erfasst: »Was brauche ich einen Baum, wenn ich die Varnay haben kann?!«

Astrid Varnay als Isolde,
Metropolitan Opera New York, 1945

Astrid Varnay als Brünnhilde, Bayreuther Festspiele 1964

Astrid Varnay, *25th April 1918 in Stockholm

She has a penchant for the dark side of human character: sinister, inscrutable guises. Consequently a favorite among her Wagnerian roles is the sly, scheming Ortrud (*Lohengrin*). Astrid Varnay recounts in her memoirs how the Bayreuth Festival conductor's children were downright frightened of meeting her backstage, so severe had she appeared in her role.

Yet Ortrud also uses her astute intelligence to take charge of her fate. Unlike Elsa, Ortrud is in need of no white knight. It is this sheer independence that impresses Varnay, who at an early age loses interest in those »innocent lambs« Elsa and Elisabeth.

Astrid Varnay achieves independence also in her own life, long before the rise of the feminist movement at the end of the 1960s. For her, a conventional life as housewife and mother is out of the question. At the same time she won't remain single. As fate would have it, she finds her ideal match in Hermann Weigert, a German-Jewish émigré who was a talented opera coach and assistant conductor at the Metropolitan Opera. In 1939 he takes the soprano under his wing as her mentor, and in 1944 they are married.

Kirsten Flagstad, a good friend of the family, serves as virtual godmother to this harmonious if childless match. She crucially sets the course of Varnay's career by her recommendations to both Weigert and the Bayreuth Festival. In the biographies of these two sopranos one finds some striking parallels: both grow up in artistic families, are instructed by their mothers in singing, begin their stage careers at an early age, and emigrate from Scandinavia to the United States, where they remain for many years.

Often the heroines' paths cross in a noteworthy way. Twice in 1951 they are cast together in *Die Walküre*: In a radio-broadcast matinee at the Met, Varnay sings Sieglinde and Flagstad Brünnhilde. A few months later at Flagstad's historic Wagnerian farewell at Covent Garden on May 31st, they switch roles. The latter performance is very special for both. In a very touching passage, Varnay recounts in her memoirs how modestly the Norwegian star unexpectedly leaves the stage to her alone during the final ovation: »All of a sudden she was no longer standing beside me, leaving for me the place she had just vacated. In a wonderfully symbolic way she seemed to say: *It is your turn – take over for me.* For me this sacred task bestowed by such a magnanimous lady was like being knighted.« [1]

Astrid's early childhood is tumultuous. Her Hungarian parents take her halfway around the globe before she is six years old – from Scandinavia through South and North America. Soon after the family arrives in New York, Astrid's father dies and she has to get a job to contribute to their living expenses. At first, she works as a secretary and earns money for her singing lessons with a side job in a bookstore.

This young singer would never in her wildest dreams have imagined that her first booking would be at the Met. At the time her first name is still Violet, but to please her agent she quickly discards it.

The soprano is just 23 years old when a golden opportunity opens up for her: When the famous Lotte Lehmann falls ill at the last moment, Varnay steps in for her and performs Sieglinde in a live radio broadcast of *Die Walküre*. The date of this unexpected, historic launch of her career is December 6th 1941.

With her commanding debut the new soprano exceeds all expectations: overnight she is the talk of the town. Yet as if that were not enough, six days later the American dramatic soprano Helen Traubel falls sick and Varnay steps in for her as Brünnhilde. The young performer feels »like Cinderella who in a flash dons a silver slipper and is saved by the prince.« [2]

From then on she masters all the great Wagnerian roles at the Met. Of all performances, her debut in 1945 as Isolde is truly nerve-wracking: Once again she steps in for Helen Traubel, but this time with considerable jitters, since she has to rehearse parts of this role in a trice.

Then in 1948, in Buenos Aires, this cosmopolitan soprano masters her first complete *Ring* Cycle as Brünnhilde.

At the beginning of the 1950s Varnay moves to Europe with her husband. Her artistic home is now, above all, the Bayreuth Festival, where she guest-stars annually from 1951 to 1968 and, like Mödl and Nilsson, becomes an institution. In later years she finds a second regular stage home at the Bavarian State Opera in Munich.

In contrast to her friend and colleague Mödl, who throws herself into her roles with the greatest conceivable intensity, Varnay does not want to lose the control. »Layer by layer« she models her characters, and curbs her natural instincts »with an analytical blueprint«. [3] And it sounds just so. Both Varnay and Mödl have dark, powerful voices, but Varnay's timbre seems somewhat cooler and, in the low range, less earthy. She has, in turn, a stronger presence in her high range, and her most beautiful sounds are her weightless head tones in the top notes.

Astrid Varnay is a cerebral person and thus rather an exception in the opera world. As Brünnhilde in *Götterdämmerung* she particularly distinguishes herself from her colleagues. She acutely parses the text: whereas Nilsson achieves her vocal conquests with her »phenomenal high notes« and Mödl attains »gravity« in her final scene like no other Brünnhilde,

Varnay's strength is in the »intensity of the dramatic scenes, especially in the passionate oath in the second act.« [4]

In her performance as Brünnhilde at the premiere of Wieland Wagner's *Ring* Cycle at the first Bayreuth Festival after the end of the war she arouses a show of enthusiasm even among the German critics. For instance, the *Süddeutsche Zeitung* reviewer recognizes her Brünnhilde as »unrivalled in her physical as well as mental mastery of the role.« [5]

The following years confirm this image: Varnay is a »phenominon of mental penetration, vocal mastery and theatrical realization of this tremendous role,« the *Süddeutsche Zeitung* once again proclaims. [6]

One of her most famous roles is without question Isolde. There are natural affinities: Varnay, like Ortrud, is able in any situation »to take the initiative without regard to the consequences of her decision.« [7]

It is a shame that the record industry has failed to immortalize Varnay's Wagnerian performances. Like many a performer, such as Ludmila Dvořáková, Varnay suffers from the fact that all labels compete with outstretched arms for superstar Birgit Nilsson. Nilsson records all of her great Wagnerian operas, and the budgets are all spent. The companies overlook the fact that it could be very interesting for future generations to compare different first-class interpretations from this era. At least »pirates« circulate several valuable live recordings of Varnay, which are now legally available.

By the end of the 1960s the career of this post-war Wagnerian heroine draws to a close. She performs her last Brünnhildes in 1970 – in Düsseldorf (*Die Walküre*) and Stuttgart (*Götterdämmerung*). Thereafter, like Mödl, she turns to character roles, and captivates her audiences in performances as Clytemnestra (*Elektra*), the Nurse (*Die Frau ohne Schatten*), Herodias (*Salome*), the Sextoness (*Jenůfa*), Leocadia Begbick (*The Rise and Fall of the City of Mahagonny*), and as the Countess in *Pique Dame*.

On December 4, 2006 Astrid Varnay dies in Munich. The authors of numerous obituaries pay tribute to her with Wieland Wagner's oft-quoted exclamation which aptly captures her down-to-earth nature: »Why do I need a tree when I can have Varnay instead?«

Birgit Nilsson, *17. Mai 1918 in Västra Karup, Schweden

»Martha Mödl war die tragische, schicksalsbeladene Isolde, Astrid Varnay war die rache-lüsterne Isolde, und Birgit Nilsson war die liebende Isolde!« So charakterisiert Wieland Wagner instinktsicher seine drei legendären Heroinen in Bayreuth. [1]

Ihre Wesenszüge korrespondieren mit ihren unverwechselbaren, markanten Stimmen. Nilssons Sopran ist heller und lichter als der ihrer Kolleginnen, dabei aber keineswegs kleiner. Im Gegenteil: Nilsson empfiehlt sich wie Kirsten Flagstad als eine nordische Naturgewalt mit enormem Volumen und schier unerschöpflichen Reserven, weshalb etliche Experten in ihr eine würdige Nachfolgerin der genialen Norwegerin sehen.

Unter den Hochdramatischen ihrer Generation ist Nilsson – stets intonationssicher in allen Registern, makellos in der Stimmführung und mit dem funkelnd schönen Timbre eines fein geschliffenen Diamanten gesegnet – wohl die Perfekteste, eine *Assoluta* des Wagner-gesangs. Besonders, wenn es vom Text her unmittelbar um die Liebe geht – wie im Duett *O sink hernieder* oder beim *Mild und leise* – betört Nilsson im *Tristan* mit einer engelsgleichen Strahlkraft.

Aber auch im *Ring* finden sich vergleichbar berührende Momente. Mit Mitleid erfüllt Brünnhilde die verbotene Liebe Siegmunds zu seiner Zwillingsschwester Sieglinde, so dass sie ihm ihre Hilfe nicht versagen kann, wie sie dem zornigen Wotan im dritten Akt der *Walküre* zu erklären versucht. *Der diese Liebe mir ins Herz gelegt* [2] ist in dieser Szene aus Nilssons Sicht die schönste Phrase. Sie »muss wirklich *bel canto* gesungen werden, und die Stimme sollte über dem Orchester schweben wie eine Feder auf dem Wasser«, fordert die Interpretin in ihren Memoiren. [3] Genau so klingt es bei ihr auch, vor allem in der grandiosen Gesamtaufnahme unter Sir Georg Solti.

Ihr Werdegang aber führt über einen recht steinigen Weg.

Zwar genießt die auf dem Lande aufwachsende Bauerntochter Nilsson im neutralen Schweden eine unbeschwerte Kindheit – verschont vom Geschehen des Zweiten Weltkriegs, Fliegeralarm und Bombenangriffen. Ein großes Problem aber sind ihre Lehrer. Mit Ausnahme eines engagierten Kantors, der sie erfolgreich auf die Aufnahmeprüfung an der Musikhochschule in Stockholm vorbereitet, gerät Birgit permanent an unfähige Pädagogen, die sie in ihrer Entwicklung eher hemmen als fördern.

Ihre letzte Mentorin schließlich, die in den 1920er Jahren für ihren Wagnergesang berühmte Nanny Larsén-Todsen, erzählt im Unterricht fortwährend nur von der eigenen Karriere. Enttäuscht zieht Nilsson einen Schlußstrich unter das Kapitel Unterricht und entdeckt für sich selbst den Kopfklang, den ihre Meister versäumten, bei ihr auszubilden.

Ein weiterer Härtetest erwartet die allen Widerständen tapfer Trotzende 1946 bei ihrem Debüt an der Königlichen Oper in Stockholm. Es ist eine Art Feuerwehreinsatz: Die Direktion bemerkt zu spät, dass sich eine Sängerin im Urlaub befindet, Birgit Nilsson soll sie kurzfristig als Agathe im *Freischütz* ersetzen. Doch welchen Tobsuchtsanfall muss die Einspringerin erleben, als ihr ein kleiner Fehler bei einer Probe unterläuft: Leo Blech, Dirigent dieser Produktion, gibt ihr unmissverständlich zu verstehen, dass er sie für »unmusikalisch und unbegabt« hält.

Es folgt eine einjährige Durststrecke an der Stockholmer Oper, während der das Energiebündel Nilsson trotz guter Kritiken vergeblich auf nennenswerte weitere Aufgaben hofft.

Dann aber bietet Intendant Harald André ihr 1947 Knall auf Fall die Lady Macbeth an. Es ist Nilssons große Chance, sie beschert endlich den ersehnten Durchbruch. Fortan ist Leo Blech ein Bewunderer ihrer Kunst, die Stockholmer Oper verpflichtet sie als festes Ensemblemitglied, und schon bald ist Birgit Nilsson – zunehmend in Wagnerpartien wie Senta, Elsa oder Sieglinde zu erleben – als veritable Nachfolgerin der beliebten Britta Herzberg in aller Munde.

Aber auch Rückschläge bleiben nicht aus. Als die Sopranistin 1949 im neuen *Ring* kurzfristig zusätzlich zur Sieglinde die *Siegfried*-Brünnhilde übernehmen soll, geraten die ersten Proben zu einem Fiasko: »Das Erwachen klappte noch ganz gut«, schreibt Nilsson in ihren Lebenserinnerungen, »aber als das Orchester mit dem Grußmotiv der Brünnhilde begann, meinte ich, die Brust müsste mir zerspringen bei diesem ungeheuerlichen Musikstrom. [...] Ich war völlig versteinert. Die paar Mal, die ich mich bemühte, den Mund zu öffnen, war es entweder zu spät oder zu früh.« [4] – Zur Premiere aber feiert die Willensstarke einen Riesentriumph: »Birgit Nilsson ist nicht nur auf dem Weg dorthin, sie ist bereits eine Wagnersängerin von Weltklasse«, lobt sie die Presse. [5]

Mitte der 1950er Jahre beginnt ihre internationale Karriere. Nach und nach gastiert Nilsson in allen großen Metropolen. Im Gepäck hat sie sämtliche Partien, die das hochdramatische Fach zu bieten hat, sowie die Donna Anna (*Don Giovanni*), *Aida* und *Tosca*. Eine begnadete Darstellerin ist sie nicht, aber das lässt ihr herrlicher Gesang vergessen. Wo auch immer sie hinkommt, fliegen dem auch geschäftstüchtigen Weltstar, der sich gerne damit brüstet, Höchstgagen auszuhandeln, Sympathie und Begeisterung zu.

1953 holt Wolfgang Wager die Primadonna auch nach Bayreuth. Hier kommt es ein Jahr später zu dem historischen Ereignis zweier Aufführungen der *Walküre*, in denen die drei Nachkriegsprimadonnen gemeinsam auf der Bühne stehen: Mödl und Varnay alternierend als Sieglinde und Brünnhilde, Nilsson in der kleineren Partie der Ortlinde. – Eine Luxusbesetzung der Extraklasse.

Nilsson tritt gegenüber dem Festspielchef sehr selbstbewusst auf, dank ihres großen Namens kann sie es sich leisten, Bedingungen zu stellen. Sie will die Brünnhilde nur in einer Neuinszenierung singen. Diese Möglichkeit bietet ihr Wolfgang Wagner 1960 in dem ersten *Ring* unter seiner Regie. Für die Sopranistin wird diese Produktion zu einem großen Triumph: »Als *Wunschmaid* oder Siegfrieds Braut – immer ist sie die Stimme jauchzender Liebe. Neben ihr zu bestehen, bedarf es der sängerischen Klugheit«, so schwärmt zum Beispiel der *Münchner Merkur* über sie. [6]

38 Jahre währt die außergewöhnliche Karriere einer Künstlerin, die dank guter physischer Kondition unzählige Male ihre gewaltigen Partien meistert und nichts so sehr scheut wie Rummel um ihren letzten Auftritt. Mehr als 200 Male verkörpert sie allein die Isolde, zuletzt noch in fortgeschrittenem Alter Anfang 60.

In ihrem Haus in Südschweden stirbt die große Wagnersängerin 2005 im Alter von 87 Jahren.

Birgit Nilsson als Isolde, Metropolitan Opera New York, 1959

Szene aus der *Götterdämmerung* mit
Birgit Nilsson (Brünnhilde) und Gottlob Frick (Hagen),
Bayreuther Festspiele 1962

Birgit Nilsson, *17th May 1918 in Västra Karup, Sweden

»Martha Mödl was the tragic, fateful Isolde, Astrid Varnay the vengeful Isolde, and Birgit Nilsson was Isolde in love!« So Wieland Wagner characterises, with unerring instinct, his three legendary heroines at Bayreuth. [1]

Her characteristic traits are reflected in her distinctive, striking voice. By comparison with her colleagues, Nilsson's soprano is brighter and more lucid, but in no way smaller. To the contrary, like Kirsten Flagstad, Nilsson is nothing less than a Nordic force of nature, with enormous volume and almost inexhaustible reserves, which is why a number of connoisseurs find in her a worthy successor to that brilliant Norwegian.

Among the high dramatic sopranos of her generation Nilsson represents the *assoluta*, the supreme Wagnerian – blest as she is with ever-constant intonation in all registers, flawless technique in voice leading, and a voice with the exquisite sparkling timbre of a finely cut diamond.

Nilsson beguiles her audience with an celestial brilliance – especially when the libretto of *Tristan* deals directly with love as in the duet *O sink' hernieder, Nacht der Liebe* (*Descend, o night of love*) and Isolde's aria *Mild und leise* (*Mildly and gently*).

Yet in the *Ring*, as well, one encounters similarly touching moments. The forbidden love of Siegmund for his twin sister Sieglinde intstills in Brünnhilde such wonder and compassion that she cannot deny him her help – as she tries to explain to the furious Wotan in the third act of *Die Walküre*. In this scene, the phrase *Der diese Liebe mir ins Herz gelegt* (*He who instilled this love in my heart*) [2] is, according to Nilsson, the most beautiful of all. It »really has to be sung *bel canto*, and the voice should float over the orchestra like a feather on water«, the soprano explains in her memoirs. [3] And she also sings it to perfection, most notably in the sublime complete recording under Sir Georg Solti.

Her career, however, starts out on a rocky road.

To be sure, growing up as a farmer's daughter in neutral Sweden she enjoys a carefree childhood, spared from the air raids and bombings of the Second World War. But her voice teachers are a big problem. With the exception of a dedicated choirmaster who successfully prepares her for admission to Stockholm's music conservatory, she is constantly beset with incompetent teachers who hinder rather than foster her development.

Finally, her last mentor, Nanny Larsén-Todsen, who was famous for her Wagnerian roles in the 1920s, talks endlessly and exclusively about her own career during the voice lessons. Frustrated, Nilsson puts an end to the classes. She discovers for herself the head voice that her teachers have neglected to cultivate.

One more acid test awaits Nilsson, who bravely overcomes all obstacles at her debut at Stockholm's Royal Opera in 1946. It is a kind of fire run: the opera management realises too late that the soprano who was supposed to sing Agathe in *Der Freischütz* is on holiday and that Birgit Nilsson, the understudy, must fill in for her at the last minute. At rehearsal Nilsson has to endure director Leo Blech's temper tantrum when she makes a minor mistake: he tells her in no uncertain terms that he thinks she is »unmusical and untalented.«

Nilsson faces a difficult first year at the Stockholm Opera, during which, despite good reviews, this live-wire soprano hopes in vain for major offers.

Then out of the blue, the general manager Harald André offers her Lady Macbeth in 1947. This at last is Nilsson's great opportunity for the breakthrough she has so long sought. From then on Leo Blech becomes an admirer of her art and the Stockholm Opera engages her as a permanent member of the company. Birgit Nilsson performs an increasing range of Wagnerian roles such as Senta, Elsa, and Sieglinde, and soon is the talk of the town as a true successor to the popular Britta Herzberg.

But there are still some setbacks. When on short notice the soprano is required to undertake, in addition to her Sieglinde, the role of Brünnhilde (in *Siegfried*) in the new 1949 *Ring* Cycle, the first rehearsals are a fiasco: »The awakening worked out just fine«, writes Nilsson in her memoirs, »but when the orchestra started to play Brünnhilde's leitmotif, I thought my breast would burst from this monstrous music-storm. […] I was totally petrified. Every time I tried to open my mouth it was either too late or too early.« [4] – At the premiere, however, the determined soprano scores a huge triumph: »Birgit Nilsson is not just on the way to becoming a world-class Wagnerian, she already is one«, the press raves. [5]

The mid-1950s mark the beginning of her international career. By and by, Nilsson is invited to guest-star in all the major houses. Her repertoire includes the most demanding roles of a Wagnerian dramatic soprano as well as Donna Anna (*Don Giovanni*), *Aida* and *Tosca*. She is admittedly not a natural actress, but her superb singing more than compensates. This most practical world-class star takes pride in negotiating top fees for herself, yet wherever she performs she arouses empathy and enthusiasm.

In 1953 Wolfgang Wagner engages her for Bayreuth. A year later she takes part in a historic pair of performances of *Die Walküre*, wherein three post-war prima donnas sing together on stage: Mödl and Varnay alternate Sieglinde and Brünnhilde while Nilsson performs the minor role of Ortlinde – a super-deluxe cast!

Birgit is very assertive with Wolfgang Wagner and, given her box-office standing, sets her own terms. She will sing Brünnhilde only in a new production. Wagner offers her his opportunity in the first *Ring* production under his direction in 1960. She scores a personal triumph: »In the part of Wotan's *Wunschmaid* (Brünnhilde) or Siegfried's bride – she is always the voice of exultant love. To measure up to her requires great vocal acumen«, raves, for instance, the *Münchner Merkur*. [6]

The illustrious career of this artist lasts thirty-eight glorious years. Thanks to her sound constitution, she is able to master her huge roles time after time and she shies away from nothing save the hype over her final performance. She performs Isolde alone more than two hundred times, the last well into her early sixties.

The great Wagnerian soprano dies at home in southern Sweden in 2005 at the age of eighty-seven.

Ludmila Dvořáková, *11. Juli 1923 in Kolin, Mittelböhmen

Tonzeugnisse gibt es nicht allzu viele von ihr, weil Mikrofone ihr verhasst sind, und die Literatur über Ludmila Dvořáková ist überschaubar. Dennoch oder gerade deswegen darf die Tschechin in diesem Buch auf keinen Fall fehlen, gilt es doch auf raren antiquarischen Aufnahmen eine prächtige, goldene, kultiviert geführte Stimme zu entdecken, dunkel in der Färbung wie Flagstad und Mödl. Nicht zufällig adeln Zeitzeugen sie als »Kronprinzessin nach Astrid Varnay und Birgit Nilsson« [1] und haben dabei allemal auch ihre zierliche Gestalt und ihre erotische Ausstrahlung im Visier.

In jungen Jahren wagt Ludmila Dvořáková, im Singen ebenso begabt wie im Klavierspiel, von einer solchen Entwicklung nicht einmal zu träumen. Sie will Modedesignerin werden und lässt sich drei Jahre lang an einer Schule für diesen Beruf ausbilden. Es ist dann ihre private russische Gesangslehrerin, die ihr musikalisches Potenzial erkennt und sie ans Prager Konservatorium empfiehlt.

Als ihre Bühnenlaufbahn am Stadttheater von Mährisch Ostrau (Ostrava) beginnt, ist Wagner in der Tschechoslowakei noch »nicht populär«. Die Frauenfiguren in Opern von Janáček, Dvořák und Mozart zählen zu den ersten Aufgaben der Debütantin, die an der kleinen tschechischen Bühne auch den Dirigenten Rudolf Vasata, ihren späteren Ehemann, kennenlernt.

Dvořákovás erste Wagnerpartie ist die Senta im *Fliegenden Holländer*, später kommt am Prager Nationaltheater die Elisabeth im *Tannhäuser* dazu.

Mit ihrem festen Engagement an die Ostberliner Staatsoper Unter den Linden, an der Dvořáková 1960 unter Franz Konwitschny als Leonore im *Fidelio* debütiert und mit ihrer dunklen Mezzofarbe auch gern als Octavian im *Rosenkavalier* besetzt wird, beginnt ihre Weltkarriere. Sie erweitert ihr Repertoire an Wagnerpartien, avanciert neben Theo Adam und Peter Schreier zu den Sendboten der Lindenoper und ist bald ein gefragter Gast an renommierten Bühnen wie der Mailänder Scala, der Londoner Covent Garden Opera, dem Teatro Colón in Buenos Aires oder der New Yorker Met. Nach München und Wien lässt sie sich vertraglich binden, ihr Heimathafen aber ist und bleibt die Ostberliner Lindenoper, an der sie politisch weitaus größere Freiheiten genießt als zuvor bei ihren festen Engagements in Prag und Bratislava.

Schon über ihre ersten Brünnhilden in Berlin gerät das Fachpublikum ins Schwärmen: »Wer hätte ihr diese jubilierenden *Hojotohos*, dies innige Vibrato der *Todesverkündigung*, diese nicht nachlassenden Singenergien bis hin zur letzten Auseinandersetzung mit Wotan-Theo Adam zugetraut«, schreibt die *Opernwelt*. [2] Und die Zeitschrift *Oper und Konzert* schwärmt: »In dieser Partie vereint die schöne Sängerin eine solche Fülle idealer Eigenschaften, dass man geneigt ist, zu Superlativen zu greifen. Allein das warme Timbre ihrer gesunden, blühenden Stimme hat Seltenheitswert.« [3]

Ähnlich bejubelt wird auch Dvořákovás Isolde: »Hier, bei dieser königlichen Maid aus irischem Geschlecht, erkannte man deutlich: [...] Des Meisters melodisch-dramatische Nuance liegt ihr im Blut und in der Kehle – jener sich mächtig entfaltende Gefühlsstrom, der keine Grenzen kennt.« [4]

Einen ihrer größten Triumphe als Isolde feiert die Sängerdarstellerin 1971 an der Londoner Covent Garden Opera unter Sir Georg Solti, den sie unter ihren Dirigenten besonders verehrt: »Dass er mich gewählt hat, war das größte Glück, das mich treffen konnte«, sagt sie, all die »herrlichen Sachen«, die er ihr beibringt, hat sie fortan immer parat, wenn sie über die Partie neu nachdenkt.

Neben ihm sind es Hans Knappertsbusch, Otmar Suitner, Karl Böhm, Joseph Keilberth und Horst Stein, denen die Tschechin musikalisch ihre wichtigsten Impulse verdankt.

Insgesamt zehn Partien aus Wagneropern erarbeitet sich Ludmila Dvořáková für ihr Repertoire, darunter auch die Kundry (*Parsifal*), die Venus (*Tannhäuser*), Sieglinde (*Walküre*) und Gutrune (*Götterdämmerung*).

Unter ihren zahlreichen Auftritten als Brünnhilde ist ihr besonders die Bayreuther *Walküre* 1967 unter Otmar Suitner mit Martha Mödl als Fricka in Bayreuth unvergessen.

Ihr Erfolg steigt ihr nie zu Kopf. Starallüren liegen der Perfektionistin fern, die zu einer aussterbenden Spezies zählt, für die Kunst noch eine Herzenssache ist. Demütig stellt sie sich in den Dienst der Komponisten, was sich vor allem zeigt, wenn man sie auf die Psychologie ihrer Figuren befragt: »Ich war hundertprozentig Wagner treu. Es steht ja alles in den Noten. Man braucht sich nichts auszudenken.«

Dvořáková will den Kopf ganz frei haben für ihre Kunst, wie Mödl ihre Energie allein dem Beruf widmen und kinderlos bleiben. Ihr langjähriger, besonders geschätzter Bühnenpartner, der amerikanische Tenor Jess Thomas, bestärkt sie in ihrer Konsequenz und spricht ihr mit seinen treffenden Worten ganz aus der Seele: »Du musst einen Kreis der Einsamkeit um dich herum schaffen und niemanden herein lassen.« – Dies umso mehr, da Ludmila Dvořáková an fürchterlichem Lampenfieber leidet und nach Ende einer Vorstellung hart mit sich ins Gericht geht. Allein die Sorge, ein Achtel zu spät eingesetzt zu haben, bereitet ihr mitunter schlaflose Nächte.

Von groß angekündigten Bühnenabschieden hält die uneitle Künstlerin gar nichts. Ganz leise sagt sie ihrem Publikum kurz vor dem Fall der Berliner Mauer adieu: »Eines Tages wusste ich, dass ich es nicht mehr schaffen würde. Ich begann, mich vor der stimmlichen Anstrengung zu fürchten, da hab ich einfach aufgehört.«

Ludmila Dvořáková als Brünnhilde,
Bayreuther Festspiele 1967

Ludmila Dvořáková als Isolde, Metropolitan Opera New York, 1967

Ludmila Dvořáková, *11th July 1923 in Kolin, Mittel-böhmen

There are not many recordings of Ludmila Dvořáková since she hates microphones, but there is enough straightforward literature about her. Consequently the Czech soprano must not be passed over in this book, especially since those rare old recordings reveal a splendid, golden, refined voice with a dark timbre reminiscent of Flagstad and Mödl. It is no coincidence that contemporary witnesses rank her as »crown princess after Astrid Varnay and Birgit Nilsson« [1], in view of her graceful figure and erotic aura.

In her youth, Ludmila Dvořáková – though equally gifted in singing and playing the piano – never dreams of such a career. She wants to become a fashion designer and trains as such for three years at school. It is her private Russian vocal coach who recognises her musical potential and commends her to the Prague Conservatory.

When her stage career begins at the city theater in Mährisch Ostrau (Ostrava), Wagner is »not yet popular« in Czechoslovakia. The female characters in Janáček, Dvořák and Mozart operas rank among this debutant singer's first assignments. She also meets her conductor Rudolf Vasata, her future husband, at the small Czech theater.

Dvořáková's first Wagnerian role is Senta in *Der fliegende Holländer* (*The Flying Dutchman*), followed by Elisabeth in *Tannhäuser*, at the Prague National Theater.

Dvořáková is given a contract at the East Berlin State Opera *Unter den Linden*, where in 1960 she makes her debut as Leonore in *Fidelio* under Franz Konwitschny; thanks to her dark mezzo timbre she is then consequently cast as Octavian in *Der Rosenkavalier,* and her international career is launched. She broadens her repertoire of Wagnerian roles, advances together with Theo Adam and Peter Schreier to join the Lindenoper's emissaries abroad, and is soon in demand as a guest performer at such renowned theaters as La Scala in Milan, London's Convent Garden, the Teatro Colón in Buenos Aires, and New York's Metropolitan Opera. She has contracts with Munich and Vienna, but her home company remains the Unter den Linden in East Berlin, where she is granted by the political authorities far more liberty than she previously enjoyed at the opera houses of Prague and Bratislava.

The music critics already wax lyrical about her first Brünnhildes in Berlin: »Who would have thought that she is capable of those jubilant *Hojotohos,* that profound vibrato of the annunciation of death, that unflagging vocal energy right up to the last confrontation with Theo

Adam's Wotan«, writes the *Opernwelt* (*Opera World*). [2] And the magazine *Oper und Konzert* (*Opera and Concert*) rhapsodizes: »In this role the beautiful soprano combines such an abundance of qualities that one must resort to superlatives. The warm timbre of her healthy, blooming voice is itself a rare treasure.« [3]

Dvořáková's Isolde is similarly hailed: »Here, in the role of the young princess of the Irish royal house, one clearly recognises that [...] the master's melodic and dramatic nuances are in her blood as well as her throat – this powerfully gathering flood of emotions which knows no bounds.« [4]

The dramatic soprano scores one of her greatest successes as Isolde at London's Covent Garden in 1971 under Sir Georg Solti, a conductor whom she holds in special esteem: »That he chose me was the best thing ever to happen to me«, she says. All these »magnificent things« he teaches her are henceforth always kept foremost in mind whenever she reflects and thinks afresh about the role.

Besides Solti, the Czech soprano owes her most important musical influences to Hans Knappertsbusch, Otmar Suitner, Karl Böhm, Joseph Keilberth and Horst Stein.

All in all, Ludmila Dvořáková masters a repertoire of ten Wagnerian roles, including Kundry (*Parsifal*), Venus (*Tannhäuser*), Sieglinde (*Die Walküre*) and Gutrune (*Götterdämmerung/Twilight of the Gods*). Among her numerous performances as Brünnhilde, the 1967 Bayreuth production of *Die Walküre* under Otmar Suitner, with Martha Mödl as Fricka, is especially dear to her memory.

Success has never turned her head. This perfectionist never puts on airs. She belongs to that endangered species for whom art is still a matter of the heart. She humbly serves the composers – a fact she most notably reveals whenever she is asked about her characters' psychology: »I was a hundred-per-cent faithful to Wagner. Everything is in the notes. One does not need to invent anything.«

Dvořáková wants to be clear-headed for her art, and, like Mödl, dedicates her energy solely to her profession – and remains childless. Her highly esteemed and long-standing partner on the stage, the American tenor Jess Thomas, supports her in her decision and offers apt words from the bottom of his heart: »You have to create a circle of solitude around you and let nobody in.« – All the more because Ludmila Dvořáková suffers terrible stage fright and at the end of a performance is hard on herself. Just the anxiety that she started an eighth note too late can cause her sleepless nights.

The modest artist thinks less than nothing of grandly announced retirements from the stage. Shortly before the fall of the Berlin Wall, she quietly bids her audience *adieu*: »One day I realised that I wouldn't be able to manage it any longer. I began to dread the vocal strain – so I simply called it quits.«

Dame Gwyneth Jones, *7. November 1936 in Pontnewynydd, Wales

Ich habe Mut! Leonores glühendes Bekenntnis im *Fidelio* wirkt wie zugeschnitten auf Gwyneth Jones, die in dieser Partie große Beachtung findet und auch im eigenen Leben der Kunst zuliebe viel auf sich nimmt.

Wahren Heldenmut legt die Sopranistin 1982 in Bayreuth als Senta im *Fliegenden Holländer* an den Tag, als sie im letzten Moment und ohne Probe einspringt: Aus beträchtlicher Höhe soll sie sich von einem hohen Plafond aus durch ein Fenster stürzen. Geblendet vom Scheinwerferlicht kann sie aber den angekündigten Wagen mit der Auffangmatratze nicht sehen. Sekundenschnell überwindet sie ihre Angst vor einem schweren – womöglich tödlichen – Bühnenunfall und riskiert den Sprung ins Ungewisse. Glücklicherweise mit gutem Ausgang.

Ein herrlicheres, kühneres Kind ließe sich wohl kaum denken. So trifft es sich ideal, dass Patrice Chéreau die unerschrockene Sängerschauspielerin 1976 für seinen grandiosen *Jahrhundertring* als Brünnhilde gewinnt. Im Premierenjahr entfacht die Produktion einen riesigen, historisch wohl einmaligen Skandal, wobei sich der Unmut der Zuschauer von Abend zu Abend unter Einsatz von Trillerpfeifen steigert. Zu Beginn des dritten Akts der *Götterdämmerung* brüllen Empörte »Vorhang runter!«, Winifred Wagner, einstige Festspielchefin in der NS-Zeit, ereifert sich, die »Irren« seien los. [1]

Die Aufgebrachten entladen ihren Zorn indes nicht nur am Regisseur, sondern auch an den Protagonisten dieser Aufführung. Auch Gwyneth Jones wird heftig attackiert: Aufgebrachte Altwagnerianer beschimpfen sie, spucken sie an, drohen gar anonym mit Mord. Sie erzürnen sich über Chéreaus Kühnheit, den *Ring* im Industriezeitalter anzusiedeln, nehmen Anstoß an dem Wasserkraftwerk im *Rheingold*, an Wotans Aufzug im Frack, an Szenen von unerhörter Gewalt: »Hagen hat Siegfried den Speer so oft brutal in den Rücken gerammt, dass das Publikum *Aufhören!* schrie«, erinnert sich Dame Gwyneth. Zudem schockierte der menschliche Blick auf die Götter, die Festspielgäste wollten nicht deren schlechte Taten sehen.

In den Folgejahren glätten sich die Wogen. Das Publikum erkennt zunehmend die Qualitäten der Produktion, Chéreau nimmt sachlich fundierte Einwände ernst, überrascht seine Kritiker mit einer intensiven Weiterarbeit an szenischen Details, bessert Schwachstellen aus und prägt mit vielen Neuerungen exemplarisch den Werkstattgedanken Bayreuths. Vor allem aber bietet er Gwyneth Jones die geeignete Plattform, ihr Potenzial als großartige Sängerschauspielerin auszuschöpfen, mit jeder Faser ihres Körpers auszudrücken, was sie fühlt.

Im Laufe des Zyklus wächst auch sie mit ihrer Figur und dem Kostüm, wie der Kritiker Reinhard Baumgart überzeugend analysiert: »Noch unter den froh leichenräumenden Walküren erscheint sie im züchtigen Graugewand als zarter, aber entschlossener Heilsarmist, eine Heilige Johanna der Schlachthöfe. Am Ende, im *Götterdämmerungs*-Gesang, hängt (sic!) sie dann in einem riesigen, weiß leuchtenden, majestätisch traurigen Vogelgewand, eine Inkarnation, so wollte es Chéreau, des Beaudelairschen Albatros: *Hemmt seinen Schritt der Riesenflügel Pracht.*«[2] Auch musikalisch empfiehlt sie sich mit strahlklaren, kraftvollen Spitzen, luziden Pianotönen, subtilen Ausdrucksnuancen, einer exquisiten Textverständlichkeit sowie einer idealen Balance von lyrischen und dramatischen Anteilen als eine erstklassige Brünnhilde. Die Videoaufzeichnung von 1979 gibt davon ein eindrückliches Zeugnis.

Um das zu erreichen, hat sich Gwyneth Jones lange Zeit gelassen, immer wieder den Bayreuther Festspielchef Wolfgang Wagner vertröstet, der sie schon 1970 in seiner *Ring*-Inszenierung als Brünnhilde gewinnen wollte. Unbeirrt geht sie ihren Weg, der stets systematisch von den kleinen Figuren zu den großen führt, im *Ring* von der Wellgunde, Ortlinde und dritten Norn zur Gutrune, Sieglinde und Brünnhilde.

Ihre erste Brünnhilde gibt Gwyneth Jones 1974 in Bayreuth nicht etwa wie die meisten Kolleginnen in *Siegfried* oder in der *Walküre*, sondern überraschend in der *Götterdämmerung*: »Da war Wolfgang ganz erstaunt. Nachdem ich nun aber die Erfahrung und die Kraft hatte, wollte ich auch die längste und schwierigste der Brünnhilden zuerst bewältigen!«

Wie manch andere Wagnerheldin beginnt auch Gwyneth Jones, 1985 mit dem *Dame Commander of the Order of the British Empire* geadelt, ihre Laufbahn als Mezzosopran. Doch schon bald nach Abschluss ihrer Lehrjahre am *Royal College of Music* und am Züricher Opernstudio entdecken namhafte Persönlichkeiten ihr dramatisches Potenzial im Sopranfach, so auch der Dirigent Sir Georg Solti, der sie 1965 in Covent Garden als Sieglinde besetzt.

Im Laufe von Jahrzehnten erarbeitet sie sich ein reiches Repertoire verschiedenster Stilrichtungen von Monteverdi über Mozart, Strauss und Wagner bis hin zu Verdi und Puccini. Sie gastiert an allen internationalen großen Bühnen und fasziniert als eine Darstellerin, die ihren Figuren stets menschlich und psychologisch tief auf den Grund geht.

Welch ein Segen, dass ihre größten Lebensleistungen als Wagner-Sängerin in Ton und Bild vorliegen: Neben dem Chéreau-*Ring* sind dies der von Götz Friedrich inszenierte, ebenfalls skandalumwitterte Bayreuther *Tannhäuser* mit Dame Gwyneth als hocherotischer, verführerischer Venus und jungfräulich schöner Elisabeth, sowie *Tristan und Isolde* in einer Produktion der Deutschen Oper Berlin, ebenfalls unter der Regie von Götz Friedrich.

Eine unübertreffliche Singenergie kennzeichnet ihre Isolde in der letztgenannten Aufführung, ihr buchstäblich lodernder Gesang treibt sie schon im ersten Akt auf den Siedepunkt. Und so inniglich wie sie mit René Kollo das Duett *Oh sink hernieder* anstimmt, vermittelt sich ihr künstlerisches Credo, das ganz ähnlich schon Martha Mödl formulierte, vielleicht stärker denn je: »Das Herz muss dabei sein, ohne Herz soll man nicht singen.«

Dame Gwyneth Jones als Brünnhilde in *Siegfried*, Bayreuther Festspiele 1977

Szene aus der *Götterdämmerung* mit Dame Gwyneth Jones (Brünnhilde), Manfred Jung (Siegfried, rechts) und Karl Ridderbusch (Hagen), Bayreuther Festspiele ˙977

Dame Gwyneth Jones, *7th November 1936 in Pontnewynydd, Wales

I have courage! Leonore's ardent confession in *Fidelio* seems to be tailor-made for Gwyneth Jones, who attracts much attention in this part and who also shoulders a lot for art's sake in her own life.

The soprano shows true valor in Bayreuth in 1982 as Senta in *Der fliegende Holländer* (*The flying Dutchman*) when she steps in the last moment without rehearsal: from a considerable height she shall throw herself from a platform through a window, but, blinded by the spotlight, she cannot see the announced cart with its back-up mattress. Within seconds she surmounts her fear of a serious or even fatal accident on stage and risks the leap into the unknown – fortunately with success.

A more superb, venturesome child could hardly be conceived. As it happens, Patrice Chéreau engages the intrepid singer and actress as Brünnhilde in his magnificent Centennial *Ring* Cycle in 1976. A production which causes an historic, perhaps unique scandal in its inaugural year: the audience's displeasure escalates night after night with the help of whistles. At the beginning of the third act of *Götterdämmerung* (*Twilight of the Gods*) the indignant audience blares »Curtain down!« Winifred Wagner, former festival director during the Nazi era, gets excited about the »psychos« running amok. [1]

The enraged crowd takes out its anger not only on the director, but also on the production's protagonists. The audience vehemently attacks Gwyneth Jones: indignant Old Wagnerians berate her, spit on her, and even shout threats of murder.

They grow enraged over Chéreau's audacity to transplant the *Ring* to the Industrial Age; they are shocked at the hydroelectric facility in *Rheingold*, at Wotan dressed in a frock coat, at scenes of untold violence: »Hagen rammed the javelin repeatedly and so brutally in Siegfried's back until the audience shouted *Stop!*«, recalls Dame Gwyneth. »Also shocking was the all-too-human view of the gods. The festival guests did not want to watch their bad behaviour.«

In the following years the waves are becalmed. The audience recognises increasingly the merits of the production. Chéreau takes informed objections seriously, surprises his critics with further work on theatrical details, mends weak spots, and in an exemplary manner and with many innovations establishes the concept of the Bayreuth workshop. Above all, he provides a suitable stage for Gwyneth Jones to exploit her full potential as a superb singer and actress who is able to express with every fiber of her being what she feels.

In the course of the cycle, moreover, she develops with the character and costume, according to critic Reinhard Baumgart's persuasive analysis: »Among the joyful corpse-collecting *Valkyries* she still seems, in her demure, gray garment, a gentle but determined Salvation Army member, a Saint Joan of the Stockyards. Singing at the end of *Götterdämmerung* (*Twilight of the Gods*), she hangs (sic!) in an huge, bright white, majestic yet plaintive bird-like garment, an incarnation, as Chéreau would have it, of Beaudelaire's Albatros: *His wings of a giant prevent him from walking.«* [2] Musically, moreover, she commends herself as a magnificent Brünnhilde with clear, vibrant high notes, lucid piano tones, subtle nuances of expression, an exquisite articulation of text, plus a perfect balance struck between the lyric and the dramatic. The 1979 video recording proves it.

To reach this pinnacle, Gwyneth Jones has allowed herself plenty of time, having staved off the Bayreuth Festival director Wolfgang Wagner, who already in 1970 wanted to engage her as Brünnhilde in his *Ring* production. Undeterred, she goes her own way – a methodical progression from minor to major characters, in the *Ring*: from Wellgunde, Ortlinde and the Third Norn to Gutrune, Sieglinde, and Brünnhilde.

She plays her first Brünnhilde in Bayreuth in 1974 – not, as with most of her colleagues, in *Siegfried* or *Die Walküre*, but surprisingly in *Götterdämmerung*: »Wolfgang was astonished. But since I already had the experience and heft, I wanted to master the longest and most difficult Brünnhilde first.«

Like many other Wagnerian heroines before her, Gwyneth Jones – knighted *Dame Commander of the Order of the British Empire* in 1985 – begins her career as a mezzo-soprano. But soon after her years of study at the Royal College of Music and the Zurich Opera Studio her dramatic potential for soprano roles is discovered by such renowned figures as conductor Sir Georg Solti, who in 1965 casts her at Convent Garden as Sieglinde in *Die Walküre*.

Over the ensuing decades she works hard at mastering a rich repertoire of distinctly varying styles: from Monteverdi to Mozart, Strauss and Wagner, to Verdi and Puccini. She guest-stars on all the major international stages and proves utterly captivating as an artist who always probes the human and psychological depths of her characters.

What a blessing that her greatest life-time achievements as a Wagnerian soprano are preserved on video: In addition to the Chéreau *Ring*, there is Bayreuth's equally scandalous *Tannhäuser*, directed by Götz Friedrich – with Dame Gwyneth as both the erotic seductress Venus and the lovely virginal Elizabeth – as well as Friedrich's production of *Tristan* at the Deutsche Oper Berlin.

In the latter performance as Isolde she displays a consummate vocal energy: by the first act, her literally blazing voice already rises to the boiling point. And so intimately does she blend with René Kollo in the love duet *Oh sink' hernieder, Nacht der Liebe* (*Oh, sink down upon us, night of love*) as she conveys her artistic credo – a credo completely in accord with Martha Mödl's : »You must put your heart into it; without the heart one should not sing.«

Hildegard Behrens *9. Februar 1937 in Varel

Heil dir, Sonne! Heil dir, Licht! Mit diesem emphatischen Gruß erwacht Brünnhilde nach langem, tiefem Schlaf. Dieser Moment ist ein Höhepunkt im dritten Akt des *Siegfried*, es ist die große Stunde der Hildegard Behrens. Mit ihrem ganzen Wesen und überirdisch schönen, strahlenden Soprantönen verkörpert sie die Heldin, die von Siegfrieds Liebesglut erfasst wird. Es ist die »Mensch- oder Frauwerdung«, wie sie es treffend ausdrückt. [1]

Ein paar Stellen in dieser langen Szene – etwa auch das *Ewig war ich, ewig bin ich* – seien »schwer schön zu singen«, meint Hildegard Behrens. [2] Dabei ist gerade sie mit ihrer außergewöhnlich hellen Stimme, die sich in den Höhen aufs Prächtigste entfaltet, eine ideale Besetzung für diese Partie.

Nur in den mittleren und tieferen Registern hat sie gelegentlich Probleme. Zu stark strapaziert sie die Bruststimme im Bemühen um größeres Volumen, kleine Kratzer und Anflüge von Heiserkeit sind die Folge. Doch darüber hört man bereitwillig hinweg.

Der New Yorker *Ring* aus dem Jahr 1990 unter James Levine – inszeniert von Otto Schenk, aufgezeichnet in Bild und Ton – belegt das künstlerische Potenzial der Sängerin in repräsentativer Weise. Er markiert – Jahrzehnte nach Leider, Flagstad, Varnay und Nilsson – ein weiteres bedeutendes Kapitel in der Aufführungsgeschichte der Met.

Behrens ist ein Energiebündel, auf der Bühne wie im eigenen Leben. Diszipliniert kämpft sie sich nach ihrem Abitur durch ein anstrengendes Jurastudium und wirkt nebenher als Mitglied des Freiburger Bachchors an ambitionierten Konzerten mit hochkarätigen Solisten mit. Dabei entdeckt sie ihre eigentliche Berufung und nimmt nach ihrem juristischen Examen noch ein Gesangsstudium auf. Ihre Laufbahn beginnt folglich erst in einem Alter, in dem manche Kolleginnen schon mit stimmlichen Krisen kämpfen. Die Sopranistin ist bereits Mitte 30 und Mutter, als ihr erstes Engagement sie 1972 an die Rheinoper in Düsseldorf führt. »Es musste immer alles gleichzeitig gehen, Beruf und Familie«, sagt Hildegard Behrens. [3] Und auf imponierende Weise schafft sie das, geht es gelegentlich auch turbulent zu wie bei einer ihrer wichtigsten Plattenaufnahmen, dem *Tristan* unter Leonard Bernstein Anfang der 1980er Jahre, während der sie mit ihrem zweiten Kind schwanger geht. Ihr Schn Philip erinnert sich, seine Mutter habe zwar für die Familie im Zuge der vielen Reisen wenig Zeit gehabt, doch beschreibt er seine Mutter als einen »unglaublich vitalen, Menschen«, der es verstand, »diese knapp bemessene Zeit ergiebig zu nutzen.«

Ihren schnellen Aufstieg verdankt die Sängerin Herbert von Karajan, der sie 1974 in Düsseldorf entdeckt und 1977 als *Salome* in Salzburg verpflichtet. Es sollte ihre Paraderolle werden, vielleicht sogar ihre größte künstlerische Leistung überhaupt, wie einige Experten meinen. Dass Hildegard Behrens zum Zeitpunkt dieser legendären Festspielpremiere schon fast 40 Jahre alt ist, merkt man ihr nicht an. Ein Zusammenspiel von vermeintlichen Widersprüchen macht ihre Figur so schillernd: Sie wirkt gleichermaßen fraulich und jung, unschuldig, verführerisch und lasziv.

War sie schon in Düsseldorf als Elisabeth, Elsa, Senta und Sieglinde in Wagners Musikdramen zu erleben, so geht sie fortan zunehmend die gewaltigen hochdramatischen Partien an – neben Isolde und Brünnhilde auch Strauss' *Elektra*. Sie bescheren ihr große Erfolge.

In Zürich kommt es am 8. Juni 1980 zu einer ganz besonderen Premiere: Hildegard Behrens und René Kollo geben gleichzeitig ihr Debüt als Tristan und Isolde in einer Inszenierung von Claus Helmut Drese unter der Leitung von Heinz Fricke. Die Sopranistin kämpft zwar im ersten Akt mit einer leichten Indisposition, doch trübt das den hervorragenden Gesamteindruck kaum. Einmal mehr bannt sie ihr Publikum mit einer sehr menschlichen Gestaltung der Rolle und besonders mit ihrem »gesanglich wunderbar fließenden *Liebestod*.« [4]

Ein großer Traum geht für Hildegard Behrens in Erfüllung, als Wolfgang Wagner sie für die Bayreuther Festspiele 1983 als Brünnhilde verpflichtet. Regelrecht »Herzflimmern« habe sie gehabt, als sie zum ersten Mal auf den Grünen Hügel fuhr, bekennt die Sängerin rückblickend im Interview mit Dieter David Scholz: »Die Brünnhilden im Theater des Meisters zum Klingen zu bringen, das war wie eine Himalaya-Besteigung für mich.« [5]

Dieser neue *Ring* gilt in vieler Hinsicht als ein historisches Ereignis: Erstmals in der Geschichte der Bayreuther Festspiele nimmt mit Sir Georg Solti ein Dirigent Umbauten an dem so berühmten Orchestergraben vor, was sich im Sinne eines lichteren, direkteren Klangbilds als durchaus vorteilhaft erweist.

Dieser *Ring*, bei dem mehrfach einige tragende Partien umbesetzt werden müssen, gestaltet sich als ein schwieriges Unterfangen. Besonders die kurzfristige Absage des Tenors Reiner Goldberg unmittelbar nach der *Siegfried*-Generalprobe trifft Solti hart.

Zu Unrecht gehen Kritiker mit dem Regisseur Sir Peter Hall und seinem Bühnenbildner William Dudley streng ins Gericht, die sich mit naturalistischen, poetischen, stimmungsvollen Bildern an Wagners originalen Szenenanweisungen orientieren. Solti hatte sich das ausdrücklich so gewünscht, ihm schwebte ein Gegenentwurf zu der »marxistischen« Interpretation Chéreaus im Sinne der musikalisch-textlichen Aussage vor. Bei ideologiekritischen Anhängern des Jahrhundert-*Rings* eckt er damit an, sie monieren das Fehlen einer Konzeption und werfen dem Regieteam mangelnde Personenführung, zahlreiche Ungereimtheiten, gar Dilettantismus vor.

Nur eine Stimme in der *Welt* begrüßt den Mut zu einer unpolitischen Deutung: »Der *Ring* ist nicht nur Menschenwerk, sondern auch ein Stück Naturgeschichte. Das hatte Chéreau völlig übersehen.« [6]

Solti nehmen die ganzen Aufregungen jedoch derart mit, dass er zur Wiederaufnahme der Produktion im Folgejahr nicht mehr antritt. Er sollte nie wieder nach Bayreuth zurückkehren.

Hildegard Behrens aber wird vom deutschen Feuilleton einhellig als Glanzlicht gefeiert. Auszugsweise sei Joachim Kaiser zitiert, dem besonders ihr »dramatisch-durchdachtes« Spiel gefällt sowie ihr »musikalisch delikater Ausdruck« in den langsamen Kantilenen beim Liebeserwachen im *Siegfried*. [7] Besonders ins Schwärmen gerät Beate Kayser in der Münchner *TZ*: »Hildegard Behrens, die Unvergleichliche, hat gezaubert. Seit der Nilsson hat keine Brünnhilde ein so hell schimmerndes Timbre gehabt. Aber die Behrens ist sensibler, weicher, verletzlicher, auch in der musikalischen Diktion, und rührt damit ganz unmittelbar an.« [8]

Leuchtende Liebe, lachender Tod: Mit einem rauschhaften Ausbruch der alles überwältigenden Liebe endet *Siegfried* und damit Hildegard Behrens' großer Auftritt. Unerwartet stirbt sie am 18. August 2009 in Tokio an einem Aneurysma. An ihre beachtlichen Lebensleistungen erinnern zahlreiche Platten und Videoaufzeichnungen.

Hildegard Behrens als Brünnhilde,
Metropolitan Opera New York, 1983

Hildegard Behrens als Isolde, Metropolitan Opera New York, 1983

Hildegard Behrens, *9th February 1937 in Varel

Hail to thee, sun! Hail to thee, light! This emphatic salutation awakens Brünnhilde after her long, deep sleep. This moment, the climax in the third act of *Siegfried,* is Hildegard Behrens's big scene. With all her being – including her extraordinarily beautiful, brilliant voice – she personifies the heroine seized by Siegfried's passion. It is her moment of »becoming human, becoming a woman«, as she aptly puts it. [1]

Some passages in this long scene – for example, the *Forever I have been, forever I am* – are »difficult to sing well«, according to Behrens [2], even though she is ideally cast in this role in which her exceptionally radiant voice soars in splendor.

Only in the middle and lower registers does she occasionally have problems. She puts too much strain on her chest voice to produce a bigger sound, but also with traces of scratchiness and hoarseness – a price her audiences readily accept.

Otto Schenk's New York production of the *Ring* in 1990 under the baton of James Levine – preserved on video – offers ample evidence of Behrens's artistic potential. It also represents – decades after Leider, Flagstad, Varnay and Nilsson – another important chapter in the performance history of the Met.

Behrens is a live wire on stage – as in life. After her graduation from high school, she manages with great discipline to combine law school with performances as part of the Freiburg Bach Choir at ambitious concerts with first-class soloists. Only after her law exams does she discover her true profession and commence vocal studies. As a result, her career starts late – at an age when many of her colleagues are already struggling with vocal crises. By the time she lands her first engagement in 1972 at the Rhein Opera in Düsseldorf, the soprano is already a mother in her mid-thirties.

»Career and family always had to be juggled«, says Behrens. [3] And she magnificently masters both, even though it is occasionally a rocky ride. For example, during one of her most important recordings – *Tristan,* under Leonard Bernstein at the beginning of the 1980s – she was pregnant with her second child. Her son Philip remembers that his mother could not spend much time with the family because of her travel schedule, but he describes her as an »incredibly energetic person« who knew »how to make the most of those rare precious moments.«

The rapid rise of Behrens's career is due to conductor Herbert von Karajan, who discovers her in 1974 in Düsseldorf and engages her to sing *Salome* in Salzburg. It is arguably her best role, perhaps even her greatest artistic performance ever, in the eyes and ears of several critics. The fact that at the time of her legendary Festival debut Behrens is almost forty years old escapes notice. It is the interplay of supposed contradictions that makes her *Salome* so iridescent: she appears at once feminine, young and innocent. yet seductive and wanton.

Already in Düsseldorf she makes her mark as Elisabeth, Elsa, Senta and Sieglinde in Wagner's operas. Then she proceeds with grand, highly dramatic Wagnerian roles such as Isolde and Brünnhilde as well as Strauss' *Elektra*. With these she achieves her greatest success.

June 8, 1980 marks the date of a very special premiere in Zürich: Hildegard Behrens and René Kollo both make their debuts in *Tristan and Isolde*, produced by Claus Helmut Drese, under the baton of Heinz Fricke. Behrens struggles in the first act with a slight indisposition, but it hardly clouds her overall brilliant performance. Once again she entrances her audience with her very human interpretation of the role and, above all, vocally with her »wonderfully fluent *Liebestod*.« [4]

Her big dream comes true when Wolfgang Wagner engages her as Brünnhilde at the Bayreuth Festival in 1983. »My heart skipped a beat« when she drove to the Green Hill the first time, Behrens confessed in hindsight in an interview with Dieter David Scholz: »To perform those Brünnhildes in the composer's own theatre was, for me, like the ascent of the Himalayas.« [5] This new *Ring* is in many respects considered historical: For the first time in the history of the Bayreuth Festival the conductor, Sir Georg Solti, makes alterations to the famous orchestra pit that result in a more lucid and direct acoustic pattern.

This new *Ring*, in which several leading roles have to be recast over and over, proves a difficult undertaking. Above all, the tenor Reiner Goldberg's last-minute cancellation immediately after the *Siegfried* dress rehearsal is a blow to Solti.

The critics unfairly castigate director Sir Peter Hall and his production designer William Dudley, who takes seriously Wagner's original stage directions for naturalistic, poetic, atmospheric imagery. Solti had explicitly requested this; by such a musical and lyrical statement he sought to create an alternative to Chéreau's »Marxist« interpretation. He upsets the ideological proponents of the Centennial *Ring*. They criticise the lack of a concept and accuse the production team of insufficient characterisations, numerous inconsistencies, and amateurishness.

Only one critic applauds their courage to pursue an apolitical interpretation: »The *Ring* is not solely a work of man, but also a piece of natural history. Chéreau completely overlooked this fact.« [6]

Solti is so upset by all the commotion that he decides not to conduct the revival of the production the following year. He never returns to Bayreuth. Behrens, however, is unanimously hailed as the highlight by the German music critics. Joachim Kaiser, for example, is especially keen on her »dramatically well thought-out« performance as well as her »musically subtle expression« in the slow cantilena at the *Liebeserwachen* (*Love's awakening*) in Siegfried. [7] As Beate Kaiser notably raves in the *Münchner TZ*: »The incomparable Hildegard Behrens has performed a miracle. No Brünnhilde since Nilsson has had such a bright, shimmering timbre. But Behrens is more sensitive, softer, more vulnerable – also in musical elocution – and therefore touches us immediately.« [8]

Radiant love, laughing death: An ecstatic burst of all-conquering love concludes *Siegfried* and therewith Hildegard Behrens's great performance. Quite unexpectedly she dies of an aneurysm on August 18, 2009 in Tokyo.

Yet her remarkable lifetime achievement is immortalized in numerous recordings and videos.

Catarina Ligendza, *18. Oktober 1937 in Stockholm

Stimme und Musikalität werden ihr von Vater und Mutter vielleicht schon in die Wiege gelegt. Und doch ist es eher die Ausnahme, dass eine Tochter berühmter Sänger selbst eine große Sopranistin wird wie Catarina Ligendza.

Um ihren eigenen Weg finden zu können, war es allerdings unabdingbar, sich aus dem dominanten Umfeld des Elternhauses zu lösen. Denn am Anfang sind Britta Herzberg und Einar Beyron, beide feste Größen am königlichen Opernhaus Stockholm, gar nicht angetan von der Idee, dass ihre Tochter Catarina ebenfalls Sängerin werden will. Beide hatten sich aus einfachen Verhältnissen hochgearbeitet, sich ihrem Beruf mit großer Hingabe gewidmet, ihn aber auch als belastend empfunden. Vor allem wenn so geniale Dirigenten wie Wilhelm Furtwängler oder Fritz Busch in Stockholm dirigierten, litten sie fürchterlich unter Lampenfieber. Ein solcher Stress sollte der Tochter erspart bleiben.

Doch Catarina nimmt heimlich ihre ersten Gesangsstunden in Stockholm, sucht beizeiten Distanz und nimmt ihr Studium in Deutschland auf. Sie träumt davon, möglichst bald die großen Frauenpartien in Wagners Musikdramen anzugehen. Ihre Lehrerin Henriette Klink-Schneider schocken solche kühnen Pläne, vertritt sie doch die verbreitete Meinung, erst ab dem 40. oder 50. Lebensjahr könne man solche Partien erwägen, anderenfalls riskiere man, die Stimme zu ruinieren. Catarina aber spürt, dass eine lyrische Partie wie die Elsa (*Lohengrin*) ihrer Stimme wunderbar entgegen kommt, lässt sich deshalb nicht davon abschrecken, sich schon in ihren Studienjahren mit ausgewählten Wagnerschen Frauenfiguren zu beschäftigen.

Es ist dann der berühmte Bassist Josef Greindl, der sie als ihr wichtigster Lehrer auf diesem Weg entscheidend fördert. Bei ihm erfährt sie, was einen »Sängerdarsteller« ausmacht. Vor allem bei der Brünnhilde legt Greindl großen Wert auf eine physische Wendigkeit: »Ich lernte es, schnell aufzuspringen, den Speer in die Luft zu schwingen, flott über die Felsen zu klettern und bei alledem die Stimme zu kontrollieren.«

Damit ist die junge Interpretin ideal gerüstet für so einmalige Regisseure wie Götz Friedrich oder Jean-Pierre Ponnelle, die sich deutlich abgrenzen von Wieland Wagners statuarisch ausgeprägtem Regiestil der 1950er und -60er Jahre. Ihre große Chance kommt, als eines Abends Astrid Varnay krankheitsbedingt für die Partie der Brünnhilde zwei *Ring*-Zyklen in Stuttgart und Berlin absagt; beide Male springt Catarina Ligendza für die ältere Kollegin ein.

Mit ihrem Engagement an die Deutsche Oper Berlin, ihre Lieblingsbühne, beginnt Anfang der 1970er Jahre ihre Weltkarriere.

Schon bald schreibt Catarina Ligendza Aufführungsgeschichte bei den Bayreuther Festspielen, setzt sie sich doch mit ihrer jugendlichen, mädchenhaften Erscheinung und ihren lyrischer ausgerichteten, erstklassigen Interpretationen deutlich ab von den hochdramatischen reiferen Parade-Brünnhilden vergangener Jahrzehnte. Entsprechend würdigen sie auch die Kritiker, die immer wieder ihren »unheroinenhaften« Typ herausstreichen.

Hinzu kommt ihre enorme stimmliche Kondition: Bei so manchen Kolleginnen lassen Kräfte und Intonation in Brünnhildes gewaltigem Schlussmonolog *Starke Scheite schichtet mir dort* auffallend nach. – Nicht bei Ligendza, die stimmtechnisch so souverän gerüstet ist, dass diese große Szene eher zu einem Höhepunkt wird: »Der Ligendza gelingt es, ihren mörderischen Part fast über die gesamte Spieldauer mit ungebrochener Stimmkraft zu durchsingen«, schwärmt etwa Norbert Miller [1] nach der Premiere von Götz Friedrichs legendärer *Zeittunnel*-Inszenierung in Berlin. Unter den Dirigenten, mit denen sie den *Ring* erarbeitet, ist es allen voran Horst Stein, von dem sich Catarina Ligendza inspiriert fühlt, seine flüssigen Tempi und subtilen Nuancierungen im Pianobereich kommen ihr sehr entgegen.

Einen engen Seelenverwandten findet Catarina Ligendza auch in dem genialen Wagnerdirigenten Christian Thielemann. Als sie ihn in den 1970er Jahren an der Deutschen Oper Berlin kennenlernt, steht er als Assistent Herbert von Karajans noch am Anfang seiner Dirigentenlaufbahn. Aber es zeichnet sich bereits ab, dass er »einmal ein ganz Großer werden würde«, empfiehlt er sich doch mit seiner subtilen Kenntnis von Wagners und Strauss' Musikdramen als »der beste Korrepetitor weit und breit.«

Besonders identifiziert wird Catarina Ligendza mit der Isolde. An ihre eigene erste unglückliche Liebe erinnert, kann sich die Interpretin in die Figur sehr gut einfühlen: »Isoldes große Liebe für Tristan ist sehr lange fast unerwidert, und das ist schmerzhaft im ersten Akt. Im zweiten Akt dagegen dominieren Glück und Jubel, dass ich manchmal sogar den Atem verloren habe beim Singen, was zur Folge hat, dass das Wiedersehen mit dem sterbenden Tristan sehr schwer zu singen ist, zumal das auch an die Nieren geht. Der *Liebestod* schließlich ist ein einziger Jubel.« Als jugendliche Erscheinung mit langem blonden Haar ist Catarina Ligendza schon äußerlich eine Isolde wie aus dem Bilderbuch, und auch musikalisch setzt sie Zeichen mit ihrer ausdrucksinnigen, über weite Strecken lyrisch angelegten Interpretation. Ihr nimmt man das Mädchenhafte der Rolle ab, zugleich besitzt sie den langen Atem, den diese Rolle erfordert. Alle drei Akte gestaltet sie stets mit gleichem Einsatz und gleicher Intensität, wobei man meinen könnte, die Sängerin Ligendza und die Bühnenfigur vereinigten sich in einer Person.

Regelmäßig spiegelt sich diese große künstlerische Leistung auch in den Rezensionen namhafter Kritiker wider. Als »eine Isolde nahe der Vollendung, eine junge, schlank-schöne, leidenschaftliche und in ihren Ausbrüchen hochdramatische Sopranistin: ein Isolden-Wunder sondergleichen«, beschreibt sie treffend Joachim Kaiser. [2] Hans Heinz Stuckenschmidt spricht von einem »Meisterstück genialer Darstellungskraft« und preist ihren *Liebestod* als »von einer seltenen Reinheit und dramatischen Ausdrucksfülle.« [3]

Auch der legendäre Carlos Kleiber ist von ihrer Isolde so ergriffen, dass er sich keine andere mehr vorstellen kann. Die Faszination beruht auf Gegenseitigkeit, sieht doch wiederum auch Ligendza in dem Dirigenten »ein Genie, weil er alles mitgestaltet«, so dass »man ihn nicht unbedingt anschauen muss, aber fühlt, dass er mitleidet, einen mitreißt in diese Klangwogen, sich verzehrt und nicht nur in der Musik aufgeht, sondern auch in jeder Rolle.«

1987 zieht Catarina Ligendza überraschend einen radikalen Schlußstrich. Sie ist zu diesem Zeitpunkt erst 50 Jahre alt, steht im Zenit ihrer Laufbahn und feiert bei ihren letzten Auftritten als Brünnhilde bei einem Gastspiel der Deutschen Oper Berlin in Tokio noch einmal große Triumphe. Die betrübliche Nachricht vom frühen Bühnenabschied trifft die Wagnerwelt folglich wie ein Schock. Doch ehrt dieser Entschluss eine weise, souveräne Künstlerin, die nicht erst abwartet bis die Kräfte nachlassen und somit ihrem Publikum in bester Erinnerung bleibt.

Probenfoto mit Catarina Ligendza
und Wolfgang Wagner,
Bayreuther Festspiele, undatiert

Catarina Ligendza als Isolde mit Yvonne Minton (Brangäne),
Bayreuther Festspiele 1974

Catarina Ligendza, *18th October 1937 in Stockholm

Voice and musicality may have been passed down by her parents but still it is rather exceptional for a daughter of famous singers to become a great soprano herself.

Yet, in order to find her own way, it was essential for Catarina to loosen the parental bonds. Britta Herzberg and Einar Beyron – both well-established members of the Royal Opera House Stockholm – were not at all keen on the idea of their daughter likewise becoming a singer. They had worked their way up from humble beginnings, dedicating themselves to their profession with great commitment, but they also found it burdensome. They suffered from dreadful stagefright when brilliant conductors like Wilhelm Furtwängler or Fritz Busch gave guest performances in Stockholm – the kind of stress they wanted to spare their daughter.

But Catarina secretly takes singing lessons in Stockholm, and in good time, seeking independence, she commences her studies in Germany.

She dreams of working on the great roles in Wagner's music dramas as soon as possible, but her teacher Henriette Klink-Schneider is shocked by such audacious plans. She shares the prevalent view that singing these parts should not be considered before the age of 40 or 50 lest they might ruin the voice.

Catarina, however, feels that a lyrical part like Elsa (*Lohengrin*) fits her voice splendidly and so she decides not to let herself be discouraged from concentrating on select Wagnerian roles in her early years of study.

Then the famous bass Josef Greindl proves to be her most important teacher in nurturing her talent in a key way. From him she learns what it means to be a singer-actress. Especially for the role of Brünnhilde, Greindl places great value on physical agility: »I learned to jump quickly, brandish the spear, jauntily climb over the rocks and all the while keep my voice under control.«

With these skills, the young singer is ideally equipped for peerless stage directors like Götz Friedrich or Jean-Pierre Ponnelle, who clearly distance themselves from Wieland Wagner's statuesque directing style of the 1950s and 60s. She gets her big chance when, owing to illness, Astrid Varnay calls off her appearances as Brünnhilde in two *Ring* Cycles in Stuttgart and Berlin. Both times, Catarina Ligendza steps in as understudy for her senior colleague.

Her engagement at the Deutsche Oper Berlin – her favourite stage – launches her international career at the beginning of the 1970s.

Soon Catarina Ligendza makes history at the Bayreuth Festival, where she distinguishes herself from the parade of highly dramatic and mature Brünnhildes of earlier decades by her youthful appearance and her distinctly more lyrical yet first-class interpretations. Accordingly, she is prized by the critics who repeatedly emphasize her »non-heroic« style.

Furthermore, she amazes everyone with her enormous vocal stamina: Many of her colleagues tend to run out of power and lose intonation during Brünnhilde's epic final monologue *Starke Scheite schichtet mir dort*, but not Ligendza. Her technical superiority allows her to turn this great scene into more of a climax. As Norbert Miller enthusiastically reports after the premiere of Götz Friedrich's legendary *Time-Tunnel* production in Berlin: »Ligendza manages to sing her blistering part with unbowed vocal power for almost the complete playing time.«[1] Among the conductors with whom she works on the *Ring*, it is Horst Stein who most inspires Catarina Ligendza. His flowing tempos and subtle piano nuances ideally suit her.

Catarina Ligendza finds another soulmate in the brilliant Wagnerian conductor Christian Thielemann. When she meets him in the 1970s at the Deutsche Oper Berlin, he is just beginning his conducting career as assistant to Herbert von Karajan, but it is already apparent that he is to become »one of the Greats« establishing himself with his in-depth knowledge of Wagner's and Strauss's musical dramas as »the best répétiteur all around.«

She is most closely identified with Isolde, with whom she can especially empathize in remembering her own first hapless love: »Isolde's great love for Tristan remains so long unrequited, and that is so painful in the first act. In the second act, however, happiness and joy are so dominant that I sometimes actually lost my breath when singing; consequently it is very difficult to sing the reunion with the dying Tristan, the moreso as this too really gets to you. The *Liebestod* is in the end a unique exultation.« As a youthful apparition with long blond hair Catarina Ligendza is on the surface an Isolde right out of a picture book, and musically she is equally exemplary with her intimately expressive and expansive lyrical interpretation. Her youthful femininity is credible but she also has the vocal stamina required for this role. She frames all three acts with the same effort and intensity whereby the singer Ligendza and the stage character effectively meld into one.

This great artistic achievement is consistently reflected in the reviews by renowned critics. She is aptly described by Joachim Kaiser as »an Isolde close to perfection, a young, slim and beautiful, passionate and in her raptures highly dramatic soprano: an unparalleled miracle of an Isolde.«[2] Hans Heinz Stuckenschmidt applauds this »masterpiece of brilliantly powerful characterisation« and praises her *Liebestod* as »of rare purity and dramatic expressiveness.«[3]

Even the legendary Carlos Kleiber is so moved by her Isolde that he can no longer imagine any other. The fascination is mutual as in turn Ligendza considers the conductor »a genius who helps shape everything in a way that there is no need to look at him to feel that he is suffering as well, sweeping you with him through these sound waves, consuming himself, immersing himself not only in the music but in every role.«

In 1987, Catarina Ligendza unexpectedly rings down the curtain. At the time she is only 50 years old, at the zenith of her career, celebrating triumphs with her last performances as Brünnhilde during a guest appearance of the Deutsche Oper Berlin in Tokyo. The sad news of her early farewell to the stage comes as a shock to the Wagner world. But this decision honours a wise and superior artist who will not wait for her powers to wane; thus she abides in the finest memories of her public.

Anja Silja, *17. April 1940 in Berlin

Mit 21 verkörpert sie ihre erste Isolde, mit 22 ihre erste Brünnhilde. Anja Silja schreibt als jüngste bedeutende Interpretin dieser Partien Aufführungsgeschichte.

Ihr Operndebüt gibt das Mädchen in einem Alter, in dem andere gewöhnlich noch die Schulbank drücken. Kurioserweise ist es ein Intendant namens Kühn, der die Fünfzehnjährige am Braunschweiger Theater engagiert, wo sie als Rosina in Rossinis *Barbier von Sevilla* debütiert. Schon bald meistert das Ausnahmetalent auch diffizile Koloraturpartien wie die Königin der Nacht in Mozarts *Zauberflöte* oder die Konstanze in der *Entführung aus dem Serail*.

Lange dauert es nicht, da hört auch Wieland Wagner von dem Wunderkind. Zwar zögert er noch nach dem ersten Vorsingen, eine so blutjunge Sängerin zu engagieren. Doch als 1960 Leonie Rysanek für den Fliegenden Holländer als Senta absagt, ist das die Stunde des Bayreuth-Debüts für Anja Silja.

Seine Zusage hat Wieland Wagner nicht bereut. Nach der gefeierten Premiere wird ihm klar, dass er mit Anja Silja einen Glücksgriff getan hat, ist sie doch mit ihrer Jugend geradezu prädestiniert für die mädchenhaften Frauenfiguren Richard Wagners, zu denen bald auch Elsa (*Lohengrin*), Elisabeth (*Tannhäuser*) und das Evchen (*Die Meistersinger von Nürnberg*) zählen.

Bald holt der an vielen Häusern wirkende Regisseur das Ausnahmetalent Silja auch an andere große Bühnen nach Berlin, Stuttgart, Brüssel, Paris, Genf, Rom oder Neapel, wo er mit ihr sogar die größten Partien erarbeitet, die das hochdramatische Fach zu bieten hat: Isolde, Brünnhilde, Salome und Elektra. Sie wird seine Muse, er ihr Mentor. Fortan sind ihre Namen untrennbar miteinander verbunden.

Fast konsequent, dass sich eine solch intensive Arbeitsbeziehung auch auf das Privatleben auswirkt. Noch nie zuvor hat sich der scheue, introvertierte, geniale Regisseur, der sich in seiner Ehe gefangen fühlt und erst kurz vor seinem Tod Mut fasst, sich aus dieser zu befreien, einem Menschen derart geöffnet. Wieland und Anja sind nicht nur Liebende, sondern auch Seelenverwandte. Und wie manche anderen komplexen Künstlerbeziehungen gestaltet sich auch diese mitunter kompliziert und belastend angesichts der schwierigen Natur eines Mannes, der »die Menschen, die er liebte, so quälte, weil er sich selbst quälte.« [1]

Sehr emotional gestaltet sich etwa die Arbeit mit Wieland am *Tristan*, wie die Sängerin in ihren Memoiren *Die Sehnsucht nach dem Unerreichbaren* ausführt: »Wir sprachen über die Figuren der Oper und wussten beide, dass wir von uns sprachen. Ich konnte nicht mehr unbefangen agieren, alles wurde persönlich und daher unmachbar für mich. Er versuchte, das zu übersehen, änderte die Szenen, wurde selbst zusehends ratloser. Die Gesten, die Emotionen entsprachen genau unseren Gefühlen [...]. Ich brach zu allem Überfluss ständig in Tränen aus, dabei krampfhaft bemüht, so zu tun, als wäre nichts.« [2]

Belasten solche Ereignisse die höchst komplizierte Beziehung auch immer wieder enorm – ihre unerschütterliche, starke Liebe macht die junge Frau stark für all die gewaltigen Aufgaben und auch für zahlreiche Bühnenskandale. Insbesondere die Interpretation der *Salome* sorgt 1964 in Paris für großes Aufsehen. Anja Silja wird mit Lolita und Baby Doll verglichen, einen vermeintlichen »Striptease in der Oper« hatte es bis dahin im ehrwürdigen Palais Garnier nicht gegeben.

Retrospektiv staunt sie, dass sie mit Wieland 36 (!) Inszenierungen in nur fünfeinhalb Jahren erarbeitete: »Das wird es auf der Welt nicht wieder geben. Die Kraft lag in der Beziehung – für keinen anderen Regisseur der Welt hätte ich das gemacht.«

Gleichzeitig fordern die physischen Strapazen aber auch ihren Tribut. Anja Silja ist gesundheitlich oft angeschlagen und muss Vorstellungen absagen. Wenn die physischen Kräfte etwas nachlassen, singt sie mitunter auch eine Spur zu tief.

Bereut hat sie diesen Einsatz nie. Im Gegenteil: Im Rückblick war ein solch anstrengendes Pensum die einzige Möglichkeit, von Wielands wertvollen Anregungen soviel wie möglich mitzunehmen, starb doch der Meister schon früh im Alter von nur 49 Jahren.

An der Schallplatte findet Anja Silja keinen Gefallen. Sie macht zwar einige Aufnahmen, doch findet sie es »schrecklich langweilig, hinter einem Mikrofon zu stehen.« Das Medium wird ihrer Persönlichkeit nicht gerecht. Man muss die legendäre Sängerschauspielerin, die mit ihrer Darstellungskraft beeindruckt wie zuvor nur wenige Andere, auf der Bühne gesehen haben.

Nichtsdestoweniger ist es bemerkenswert, was die junge Interpretin rein stimmlich leistet. Schon das enorme Volumen beeindruckt, zumal sie nicht forciert. Siljas Spitzentöne besitzen immer Substanz, grelle Schreie kommen ihr nicht unter. Und noch etwas zeichnet ihre Wiedergaben entscheidend aus: Sie spart ihre Kräfte nie für die gefürchteten großen Szenen und Monologe auf, singt vielmehr von Anfang an mit vollem Einsatz, wovon man sich besonders beim ersten Akt des 1965 in Rom aufgezeichneten *Tristans* unter André Cluytens überzeugen kann. Angesichts dessen wundert es allerdings auch kaum, dass sich Kritiker um die Zukunft der jungen Frau sorgen. Vor allem in jüngerer Zeit erlebt man es immer wieder, dass vielversprechende Wagnerstimmen oftmals schon innerhalb eines Jahrzehnts ausleiern, gar kaputt gehen. Anja Silja mag dabei sehr ihre Technik zugute kommen, die sie ihrem Großvater verdankt, ihrem ersten und einzigen Gesangslehrer. Analysieren oder beschreiben kann sie diese allerdings nicht, sie ist ihr unbewusst: »Ich muss über die Technik nicht nachdenken, würde sie auch nicht weitergeben können, sie ist einfach da.«

1963 verkörpert Anja Silja in Neapel und Köln die Brünnhilde in der *Walküre*. Wieland beschäftigt sich in diesem Werk besonders tiefgehend mit der Psychologie des komplizierten Verhältnisses zwischen Wotan und Brünnhilde, Vater und Tochter, wobei auch hier wie im *Tristan* Analogien zur persönlichen Beziehungsgeschichte zwischen Sängerdarstellerin und Regisseur hineinspielen. Entscheidend ist, dass sich gerade in Brünnhildes vermeintlichem Ungehorsam ihre starke Vaterliebe ausdrückt. Letztlich erfüllt sie Wotans geheimen, uneingestandenen Willen, seinen geliebten Wälsung Siegmund zu retten.

Zwei Textstellen aus dem dritten Akt der *Walküre* rühren Anja Silja bis heute regelrecht zu Tränen: *Der mir diese Liebe ins Herz gelegt* [3] und *zu lieben, was Du geliebt*. Sie geben ihr, erst recht nach Wielands Tod, das Gefühl, einen Dialog mit dem Mann zu führen, der alles für sie war: Liebhaber, Lehrmeister, Freund, Partner und Übervater. Noch zwei weitere Male nach seinem Tod ist die Sopranistin 1967 in Inszenierungen Wielands als Brünnhilde in der *Walküre* zu erleben: bei einem unvergessenen Bayreuth-Gesamtgastspiel in Osaka und in Paris. Ein letztes Mal schließlich tritt sie in dieser Partie 1968 in Genf auf, Regie führt hier Herbert Graf.

Szenisch nicht verkörpert hat Anja Silja die Brünnhilde in der *Götterdämmerung*. Den großen Schlussmonolog *Starke Scheite schichtet mir dort* aber beherrscht sie, wie einem kostbaren, leider längst vergriffenen Mitschnitt eines Konzerts in Helsinki aus dem Jahr 1971 zu entnehmen ist. Es macht Staunen, mit welchen enormen Reserven sie diesen meistert, wie sicher und kraftvoll sie die Spitzentöne ansetzt, die nie ins Schrille entgleisen. Eine sensationelle Wiedergabe!

Ähnliches lässt sich über Anja Siljas Isolde im 1965 aufgezeichneten *Tristan* aus Rom sagen. In ihrem Buch zitiert sie aus einer treffenden Rezension: »Die Stimme dieser jungen Sängerin besitzt nichts von der Herbheit, die man oft bei nordischen Stimmen findet, sie sprudelt klar, weich, geschmeidig, blitzend im hohen Register, sanft und einschmeichelnd im Piano.« [4]

In Interviews betont Anja Silja immer wieder, dass der Lebensabschnitt an der Seite von Wieland Wagner ihr wichtigster war. Doch geht es nach Wielands Tod irgendwie hoffnungsvoll weiter. Es ist der berühmte Dirigent André Cluytens, ein Freund Wieland Wagners, der ihr mit seiner großen Liebe emotionalen Halt gibt. Leider währt dieses Glück nicht lange. Cluytens erkrankt an Krebs und stirbt ein Jahr nach dem Wagnerenkel.

Einzig Siljas spätere Beziehung mit dem Dirigenten Christoph von Dohnányi mündet in einer Ehe – mit drei Kindern. Sie scheitert wie so viele Künstlerehen, nach über 20 Jahren.

In reiferen Jahren wechselt Anja Silja wie Mödl und Varnay ins Charakterfach. Unvergessen sind ihre Küsterin in Janáčeks *Jenůfa* sowie die 300 Jahre alte Emilia Marty in *Die Sache Makropoulos*, nach eigenen Aussagen ihre Lebensrolle. Entgegen den Meinungen einiger Kritiker, die ihr in jungen Jahren ein schnelles Ende ihrer Laufbahn prophezeiten, meistert Anja Silja noch mit Anfang 70 kleinere anspruchsvolle Rollen.

Es ist eine einmalig lange Sängerkarriere, eine Sensation. Im Wagnerfach aber hat sie sich nach Wielands Tod konsequent rarer gemacht. Nach Bayreuth kehrte sie nie wieder zurück.

Anja Silja als Elisabeth im *Tannhäuser*,
Bayreuther Festspiele 1962

Anja Silja als Brünnhilde mit
George London (Wotan)
in der *Walküre*, Oper Köln 1963

Anja Silja, *17th April 1940 in Berlin

At 21 years of age she sings her first Isolde, at 22 her first Brünnhilde. Anja Silja makes history as the youngest major performer of these roles.

The girl makes her début at an age when most of her contemporaries are still going to school. Curiously enough, it is a theater manager named Kühn – which means »brave« – who takes a chance on the fifteen-year-old at the theater of Braunschweig, where she débuts in 1956 as Rosina in Rossini's *Il barbiere di Siviglia* (*The Barber of Seville*). Soon the exceptional singer also masters difficult lyrical coloratura roles, such as the Queen of the Night in Mozart's *Die Zauberflöte* (*The Magic Flute*) and Konstanze in *Die Entführung aus dem Serail* (*The Abduction from the Seraglio*).

Shortly thereafter, Wieland Wagner hears about the prodigy. After her first audition he is still unsure whether to hire a singer of such tender years. But when Leonie Rysanek cancels her engagement as Senta in *Der fliegende Holländer* (*The Flying Dutchman*) in 1960, the time comes for Anja's début at Bayreuth. Wieland Wagner never regrets having engaged her. After a widely acclaimed opening night he realizes that he has made a fortuitous choice. Being so young, Anja is ideally suited for Richard Wagner's youthful leading roles such as Elsa (*Lohengrin*), Elisabeth (*Tannhäuser*) and Eva (*Die Meistersinger von Nürnberg*). Wieland, who works with several companies, brings Anja to other opera houses in Berlin, Stuttgart, Brussels, Paris, Geneva, Rome and Naples, where he prepares her for the greatest dramatic roles of Wagner and Strauss: Salome, Isolde, Brünnhilde and Elektra. She becomes his muse, he her mentor. From then on, their names are inseparably linked.

Their intense working relationship also affects their private lives. Never before has the shy, introverted and brilliant director opened up to another person in such a way. Wieland feels trapped in his marriage and breaks free from it only shortly before he dies; he and Anja become not just lovers but kindred spirits. Like so many relationships between artists, theirs is a complex, intricate and stressful liaison, owing to the difficult character of a man who would »plague those he loved because he plagued himself.«[1]

Her collaboration with Wieland on *Tristan and Isolde* for instance becomes very emotional as the soprano recounts in her memoir *Sehnsucht nach dem Unerreichbaren* (*Yearning for the Unattainable*): »We talked about the characters in the opera but we both knew that we were talking about ourselves. I couldn't act unselfconsciously anymore; everything became personal and therefore impossible for me. He tried to ignore it; he would change the scenes and grow more and more perplexed. The gestures, the emotions corresponded exactly to our feelings [...] On top of that I regularly burst into tears and desperately tried to pretend that nothing was wrong.« [2]

Although these events put a strain on Anja's highly complicated relationship with Wieland, her deep, unshakeable love strengthens the young woman for her great future challenges and several scandalous performances. Above all, the Paris production of *Salome* in 1964 causes a great furore. Anja Silja is compared with Lolita and Baby Doll: such a would-be »striptease in the opera« had never before been staged in the dignified *Palais Garnier*.

In retrospect, she is amazed that she and Wieland completed no fewer than 36 productions in only five-and-a-half years. »This will never happen again. My power was generated by our relationship – I wouldn't have done it for any other director in the world.« At the same time, the physical demands take their toll. Anja is frequently in poor health and therefore often forced to cancel performances. When exhausted, she even tends to sing a bit flat. Yet she never regrets being so committed. The ambitious workload was a unique chance to profit from Wieland's invaluable input as long as possible. The master dies young, at the ripe age of forty-nine.

Anja Silja does not like records. She does, to be sure, make some recordings, but she finds it »terribly boring« to stand behind a microphone. The medium does not meet the needs of her personality. The legendary Wagnerian singer is at her best onstage. Her superb acting is second to none among her peers. On top of everything, the power of her voice is terrific. The sheer volume of it is amazing, all the moreso as she has no need to force it. Anja's top notes are substantial; harsh shrieks are not in her nature. Never does she save her strength for major dramatic scenes and monologues. From the onset she sings with utmost power, proof of which may be found in listening to her *Tristan*, recorded in 1965 in Rome under André Cluytens.

In view of her intensity, it is not surprising that critics worry about the young woman's future. Especially in recent times, promising Wagnerian voices have worn out or have simply broken. Anja may have profited by her technique, which she owes to her grandfather, her first and only singing teacher. Yet she cannot analyse or describe that technique; she calls it an unconscious act. »I never think about my technique, I wouldn't be able to pass it on – it's simply there.«

In 1963, Silja sings Brünnhilde in *Die Walküre* in Naples and Cologne. In this work Wieland concerns himself deeply with the complicated psychological relationship between Wotan and Brünnhilde, father and daughter. As in *Tristan*, analogies may be found in the personal history between this singer-actress and her director. Most notably, Brünnhilde expresses her strong love for her father by her apparent disobedience. She threreby tries to fulfill Wotan's secret, unacknowledged wish to save his beloved Wälsung son Siegmund. To this day, two passages from the third act of *Die Walküre* (*The Valkyrie*) move Anja to tears: *Wer diese Liebe mir ins Herz gelegt* (*He who kindled this love in my heart*) [3] and *zu lieben was du geliebt* (*to love what you once loved*). Particularly in retrospect these passages feel like a dialogue with the man who was once everything to her: lover, instructor, friend, partner and father figure.

After his death she performs this role twice in 1967 in Wieland's stagings: In Paris and – as part of a memorable guest-performance of the complete Bayreuth program – in Osaka. Her final Brünnhilde (again in *Die Walküre*) is in 1968 in Geneva, under the direction of Herbert Graf.

Anja never gets to play Brünnhilde onstage in *Götterdämmerung* (*Twilight of the Gods*). But she masters Brünnhilde's great Immolation Scene *Starke Scheite schichtet mir dort*, as demonstrated in a precious but out-of-print recording of a Helsinki concert from 1971. It is amazing how resourcefully she masters the part, how confidently and powerfully she sings her top notes without growing shrill. A sensational rendition!

Anja's Isolde from *Tristan*, recorded in 1965 in Rome, is similarly astounding. In her book, she quotes from a telling review: »In the voice of this young singer there is not a single trace of that acerbity found very often among Nordic voices. It effervesces clearly, softly, smoothly, sparkling in the high register, gentle and mellifluous in the piano passages.« [4]

In interviews, Anja continually points out that her time with Wieland Wagner was the most important part of her career. But somehow it goes on with some hope after Wieland's death. It is the famous conductor André Cluytens, a friend of Wieland Wagner, whose great love now offers her emotional security. Unfortunately this happiness is short-lived. Cluytens is stricken with cancer and dies a year after Wagner. Only Anja's later relationship with the conductor Christoph von Dohnányi leads to marriage – and three children. Yet like many marriages between artists, it breaks down after more then 20 years.

Anja modulates into character roles as she grows older – like Mödl and Varnay. Her Kostelnicka, the Sextoness in Janáček's *Jenůfa,* is unforgettable, as is the three-hundred-year-old Emilia Marty in *Die Sache Makropoulos* (*The Makropoulos Case*), which is, by Anja's own account, the role of her life.

Contrary to the views of several critics, who predicted a swift end to her youthful career, Anja still masters – into her seventies – smaller yet demanding roles. It is a singularly long career for a singer – a sensation! Only of Wagner does she sing less and less after Wieland's death. She never again returns to Bayreuth.

Deborah Polaski, *26. Mai 1949 in Richland Center, Wisconsin

Sie ist eine der bedeutendsten Hochdramatischen ihrer Generation, entdeckt ihre Faszination für Richard Wagner aber auf Umwegen. Schwierige Jahre des Experimentierens halten Deborah Polaski auf.

Ihr erster Lehrer gibt der 18-Jährigen die Möglichkeit, ihre Stimme durch viel Koloratur-Repertoire vorsichtig zu entwickeln, die zweite Pädagogin ist mit einer Einschätzung von Polaskis stimmlichen Möglichkeiten überfordert: »Sie wusste nicht, ob ich Pamina, Mimi oder die Turandot singen soll und ließ mich alle diese Partien einstudieren«, erinnert sich die Sopranistin. – Eine Entscheidung, über die vermutlich andere Kolleginnen den Kopf schütteln würden, handelt es sich doch vor allem bei Puccinis *Turandot* um eine höchst anspruchsvolle Rolle, mit der selbst gestandene Interpretinnen lange warten.

Und auch bei ihren ersten Engagements an kleineren deutschen Bühnen singt sich die Berufsanfängerin noch querbeet durch ein illustres Rollenspektrum.

In Bayreuth hat die lange Orientierungsphase endlich ein Ende. In dem Dirigenten Daniel Barenboim und dem Regisseur Harry Kupfer, mit denen sie 1988 ihren ersten *Ring* dort einstudiert, findet Polaski mehr als ideale Partner. Sie sind es, die der Sopranistin als passionierte Wagnerianer die Tetralogie subtil erschließen wie noch niemand zuvor.

Harry Kupfer arbeitet intensiv mit ihr an der Auslegung der Texte, Barenboim sensibilisiert die Spätzünderin für Feinheiten der Interpunktion. Wagners Vorliebe gilt dem Doppelpunkt, der stets Bekenntnisse von großer Tragweite und Bedeutung ankündigt. Zwar gerät diese *Ring*-Produktion nicht zu einem großen Wurf wie *Der Fliegende Holländer*, den Kupfer so überzeugend als Sentas Traum deutete. Deborah Polaski aber weckt mit ihrem allemal respektablen Debüt Hoffnungen für die Zukunft. Sie wirkt schlafwandlerisch sicher, organisch eins mit ihrer Rolle und vor allem auch zuverlässig im Durchhaltevermögen. Unter den Kritikern zeigt sich etwa auch Joachim Kaiser beeindruckt, der ihr »stolzes Temperament«, ihre »große Ausdrucksintensität« und ihre »schöne Mittellage« hervorhebt. [1]

1989 kommt die Karriere zwar unerwartet ins Stolpern, als sich die gläubige Christin für eine Sinnsuche ins Private zurückzieht. Doch als sie 1991 in den Kupfer-*Ring* zurückkehrt, hat sie sich schon unersetzbar gemacht. Das Publikum weiß, was es an ihr hat!

Noch einmal in Alfred Kirchners so genanntem Designer-*Ring* verkörpert Deborah Polaski von 1994 bis 1998 unter James Levine die Brünnhilde in der Wagnerstadt Bayreuth. Ihn prägt weit mehr noch als der Regisseur die Kostümbildnerin Rosalie, die mit ihrer fantasievollen Ausstattung Akzente setzt. Die weiten Röcke und schweren Korsetts erfordern eine sehr reduzierte körperliche Bewegung, der Polaski etwas abgewinnen kann, muss man doch »noch präziser mit dem Text umgehen.«

Einen bemerkenswerten Rekord stellt Deborah Polaski statistisch auf: In 24 (!) *Ring*-Zyklen ist sie die Brünnhilde in Bayreuth, auf so viele Vorstellungen in dieser Partie an diesem Ort kommt sonst keine andere.

Die künstlerische, fruchtbare Zusammenarbeit mit Daniel Barenboim und Harry Kupfer aber setzt sich in Berlin fort: Erstmals 1996 holt der Chefdirigent der Berliner Staatskapelle sie wiederum als Brünnhilde zur Eröffnung der ersten Berliner Festtage an die Lindenoper. Die Stimme ist inzwischen noch größer geworden, die 47-Jährige steht im Zenit ihrer Karriere.

Unvergessen ist vor allem Kupfers *Tristan* (2000) mit einer überlebensgroßen Skulptur eines gefallenen, seinen Kopf in seinen Armen verbergenden Engels im Zentrum der Bühne – ein schlichtes wie eindrucksvolles Sinnbild der zu Grabe getragenen Liebe als einer Utopie.

Hart, kalt, grausam, aber auch zärtlich und verwundbar: Polaskis Isolde ist gleichzeitig eine starke Frau und ein hilfloses Mädchen, manche Kritiker wollen sogar eine Megäre in ihr sehen, eine »Penthesilea der Opernbühne.« [2]

Am treffendsten aber bringt es wohl der dienstälteste Feuilletonist Klaus Geitel auf den Punkt, wenn er konstatiert, Polaski verschränke »auf die nur ihr eigene geheimnisvolle Weise Würde und Weichheit zu einer Art femininer Mythologie.« [3]

Was das Bühnenbild angeht, so musste man es »genau erforschen, es war auf jede Note choreografiert, da durfte nichts dem Zufall überlassen bleiben«, bilanziert Polaski. Vielleicht ist es unter all ihren Arbeiten nach ihren eigenen Worten deshalb eine der schönsten.

Deborah Polaski als Brünnhilde,
Bayreuther Festspiele 1995

Deborah Polaski als Isolde, Staatsoper Berlin im Jahr 2000

Deborah Polaski, *26th May 1949 in Richland Center, Wisconsin

She is one of the most outstanding dramatic sopranos of her generation; yet she discovers her fascination for Richard Wagner in a roundabout way, as difficult years of experimentation hold her back.

Her first teacher gives the eighteen-year-old Deborah Polaski the opportunity to develop her voice carefully through a coloratura repertoire. Her second teacher is out of her depth in evaluating Polaski's vocal capabilities. »She did not know whether I should sing Pamina, Mimi or *Turandot,* so she let me study all three roles«, the soprano recalls – a decision other colleagues would probably not applaud. Puccini's *Turandot,* above all, is a most ambitious role that even seasoned performers wait long before tackling.

Furthermore, in her first engagements at small German opera houses the young professional indiscriminately sings a glittering range of roles.

In Bayreuth her long process of orientation comes to a close. Polaski finds her ideal partners in the conductor Daniel Barenboim and director Harry Kupfer, with whom she rehearses her first *Ring* cycle in 1988. Together – as no one has before – they subtly open up the *Ring* to the soprano as a dedicated Wagnerian.

Harry Kupfer and Polaski work intensively on text interpretation, while Barenboim raises the late bloomer's awareness of the subtleties of punctuation. Wagner prefers to use colons to announce confessions of great import and significance. To be sure, this production of Wagner's *Ring* is not as successful as *Der fliegende Holländer,* (*The flying Dutchman*) which Kupfer convincingly interprets as Senta's dream.

However, Deborah Polaski kindles expectations with her entirely respectable debut. She projects utmost confidence, achieves a total identification with the role and, above all, displays solid stamina. Joachim Kaiser, among other critics, is impressed by her »proud temperament«, her »expressive intensity« and her »beautiful middle register.« [1]

Her career admittedly flounders unexpectedly when in 1989 the devout Christian withdraws into her personal search for meaning. But when she returns, two years later, to the Kupfer *Ring* in 1991 she has already made herself indispensable. The audience knows indeed what they have in her!

Between 1994 and 1998 Polaski again sings Brünnhilde in Alfred Kirchner's so-called Designer *Ring* under James Levine in Wagner's city of Bayreuth. Costume designer Rosalie, who emphasizes fanciful accoutrements, influences Polaski even more than the director.

Polaski appreciates those ample skirts and heavy corsets which necessarily restrict physical movement and thus require her to »treat the text even more precisely.«

Deborah Polaski establishes a remarkable statistical record: she sings Brünnhilde in 24 (!) *Ring* cycles at Bayreuth – an all-time record for singing that role at that site.

The artistically fruitful collaboration with Daniel Barenboim and Harry Kupfer, moreover, continues in Berlin: In 1996 the chief conductor of the Berliner Staatskapelle initially hires her once again as Brünnhilde for the opening of the first Berlin Festival at the Lindenoper. Her voice has meanwhile grown even stronger as the 47-year-old reaches the zenith of her career.

Most memorable of all is Kupfer's *Tristan* (2000) with its larger-than-life sculpture of a fallen angel burying its head in its arms: a stark and striking symbol of love laid to rest as a utopian dream in the center of the stage.

Hard, cold, cruel but also tender and vulnerable: Polaski's Isolde is simultaneously a strong woman and helpless girl. Some critics even want to see in her a fury , a »Penthesilea of the opera stage.« [2]

However, it is the senior-most columnist Klaus Geitel who indeed gets to the heart of the matter when he states that Polaski interweaves, »in her singular and mysterious way, dignity and tenderness into a kind of feminine mythology.« [3]

Apropos of the staging, »one had to scrutinize it because it was choreographed on every note and with nothing left to chance«, Polaski recognises. Perhaps that is the reason why among all her works this Isolde is, in her own words, one of the most beautiful.

Waltraud Meier, *9. Januar 1956 in Würzburg

Die Isolde ist ihre Lebensrolle. Waltraud Meier verkörpert diese Figur mit jeder Faser ihres Seins, gerüstet mit einer strahlend kraftvollen Stimme und einem Timbre, das geradezu einmalig Erotik und Noblesse vereint.

Unzählige Male gestaltet sie diese Partie in den unterschiedlichsten Inszenierungen auf allen großen Bühnen der Welt. Doch so unterschiedlich die Konzeptionen der Regisseure auch ausfallen mögen – in ihren markanten Wesenszügen bleibt Waltraud Meiers Isolde stets unverwechselbar.

Ihre Laufbahn beginnt nach einem privaten Gesangsstudium im Alter von 20 Jahren am Stadttheater in Würzburg als Mezzosopran. Dieses Fach wird sie – auch wenn sie später ihr Repertoire mit ausgewählten dramatischen Sopranpartien aufstockt – nicht aufgeben.

Sehr individuell entscheidet sie von Zeit zu Zeit, welche Rollen für ihre Stimme infrage kommen. Nomen est omen, und so ist es vielleicht kein Zufall, dass die Waltraute (Götterdämmerung) zu Waltrauds ersten Wagnerfiguren zählt – eine Partie, die sie seither über 30 Jahre begleitet.

Dass sie sogar an einem einzigen Abend flexibel zwischen unterschiedlichen Stimmfächern und konträren Rollen grandios zu changieren vermag, zeigt sich 2002 bei einer unvergessenen, singulären, fast kuriosen Walküre in der Berliner Staatsoper, bei der sie nach der kurzfristigen Absage einer Kollegin Sieglinde und Fricka im Doppelpack meistert.

Zu den Paraderollen der famosen Wagnerheldin zählt unzweifelhaft die Kundry, verschmelzen doch bei ihr Gesang, Darstellung und äußere Erscheinung zu einer idealen Einheit. Zudem mit Spitzentönen gerüstet, die Leuchtraketen gleichen, übertrifft sie 1983 bei einem schier sensationellen Debüt in Bayreuth jegliche Erwartungen. Fortan ist sie konkurrenzlos die Nummer Eins unter den Interpretinnen dieser Partie.

Überhaupt gibt es unter all ihren Figuren keine, die Waltraud Meier vom Wesen her fremd wäre, noch nicht einmal die fiese Ortrud im Lohengrin. Sie müsse nur tief in ihre Heldinnen »hineinkriechen«, sagt die Künstlerin, dann könne sie bestens mit ihnen fühlen. Ohne ein solch starkes Einfühlungsvermögen würde sie bei ihrem ersten Tristan 1993 in Bayreuth vielleicht auf verlorenem Posten stehen, kommen doch von ihrem Regisseur Heiner Müller in punkto Personenführung »so gut wie keine Impulse.« Atmosphärisch stark wirkt diese Produktion gleichwohl dank den geometrisch klar umrissenen Bühnenräumen von Erich

Wonder sowie raffinierten Beleuchtungswechseln und vornehmen, futuristischen Designer-kostümen. Der größte Trumpf aber – und für den Kritiker der *Zeit* auch »die eigentliche Über-raschung« dieser Aufführung – ist Waltraud Meier: »Die Vielseitigkeit ihrer Stimme ist enorm, jeder Ton ist wohlkalkuliert und schwingt frei. Eine bessere Isolde ist derzeit kaum denkbar, auch deshalb, weil sie als Persönlichkeit von so überzeugender Intensität ist.« [1]

Dieser Bayreuther *Tristan* fokussiert ganz und gar auf die Unmöglichkeit einer erfüllten Liebe. Deshalb spielt der zweite Akt auch nicht an einem lauschigen Ort einer »hellen, an-mutigen Sommernacht«, wie in Wagners Textbuch angegeben, sondern in einer Rüstkam-mer mit aufgereihten Harnischen als Signum einer waffenstarren Männerwelt. Publikum und Presse spaltet diese ganz und gar auf Abstraktion zielende Interpretation, die nur selten eine körperliche Nähe zwischen den Figuren zulässt. Bei aller szenischen Nüchternheit sorgen aber allen voran Waltraud Meier und Daniel Barenboim dafür, dass diese erotischste, oszil-lierende Musik, die je geschrieben wurde, zu ihrem Recht kommt. Oft schlagen Funken zwi-schen Bühne und Orchestergraben.

»Wir sind wie Hand und Handschuh, nur weiß ich nicht, wer was ist«, soll Barenboim später einmal gesagt haben, nachdem Waltraud Meier und er zahlreiche Aufführungen ge-meinsam gemeistert haben. Worte, die sehr zärtlich und treffend ihrer langjährigen engen, fruchtbaren künstlerischen Partnerschaft Ausdruck geben.

17 Jahre lang schreibt Waltraud Meier als Kundry, Isolde und Waltraute Bayreuther Festspiel-geschichte, dann kommt es zu einem Bruch. Ihre Differenzen mit Wolfgang Wagner resultie-ren aus der geforderten strikten Präsenzpflicht in der Probenzeit: Noch für eine andere Partie in München unter Vertrag, bittet Meier um Freistellung an einigen Tagen – Wagner will keine Ausnahme machen.

Als Sieglinde in der von Giuseppe Sinopoli dirigierten Neuproduktion des *Rings* verab-schiedet sich Waltraud Meier im Jahr 2000 von Bayreuth. Dieses Zerwürfnis aber ist für sie längst eine Marginalie geworden, zumal Wagner und sie sich wenig später untereinander wieder »ausgesöhnt« haben. Die vielen Jahre, die sie in Bayreuth mit »wunderbaren Kolle-gen« wie im »Kreis einer Familie« verbrachte, zählt sie zu »den schönsten ihres Lebens.«

Unter all ihren *Tristan*-Regisseuren hebt die Interpretin Patrice Chéreau hervor, dessen fein psychologisierte Inszenierung 2007 an der Mailänder Scala herauskommt, einmal mehr mit Daniel Barenboim am Pult. Sie ist begeistert von »seiner Art, menschliche Schicksale dar-zustellen«, dankbar dafür, dass er im Gegensatz zu so manchen anderen Regisseuren jeden Satz und »das Zusammenspiel der Figuren untereinander auf der Bühne zu Ende denkt.«

Somit hat sie Gelegenheit, die wechselnden Emotionen dieser komplexen Figur – Ver-zweiflung, Rachsucht, Begehren und Todeswillen – bis in kleinste Nuancen auszuleuchten.

Publikum und Presse feiern sie dafür gleichermaßen. Die Kritikerin der *FAZ* etwa schwärmt von einer »immer noch herrlich ungestümen, zugleich bewundernswert artikulationsklar und intonationssicher gestaltenden Waltraud Meier«, zeigt sich im Szenischen vor allem beeindruckt von dem Moment im ersten Aufzug, wenn Tristan und Isolde »magnetisiert zueinander finden, sich verschmelzungssüchtig aneinander klammern, schließlich gewaltsam von Brangäne getrennt werden.« [2]

Die Brünnhilde macht Waltraud Meier nicht zu ihrer Partie. Sie würde es vermutlich doch erfordern, sich zu weit von dem angestammten Mezzofach zu entfernen, das täte ihr nicht gut. Immerhin stellt sie sich für ein Wagner-Album der Herausforderung des Schlussgesangs aus der *Götterdämmerung*, und der gelingt ihr in jeder Hinsicht einfach trefflich. Ihre Lebensrolle aber ist und bleibt die Isolde.

Szene aus *Tristan und Isolde* mit Waltraud Meier (Isolde), Siegfried Jerusalem (Tristan) und Falk Struckmann (Kurwenal, hinten), Bayreuther Festspiele 1999

Waltraud Meier als Isolde,
Teatro alla Scala, Mailand 2007

Waltraud Meier, *9th January 1956 in Würzburg, Germany

Isolde is the role of her life. Waltraud Meier embodies this character with every fiber of her being – equipped with a radiant and powerful voice and a unique timbre that combines eroticism and noblesse.

Time after time she interprets this part in a wide variety of productions on all the great international stages. No matter how varied the conceptions of the directors, her Isolde always bears her own distinctive traits.

Following private vocal studies, she begins her career as a mezzo-soprano at the age of 20 at the city theater in Würzburg. While she never abandons her mezzo roles she later augments her repertoire with select dramatic soprano parts.

From time to time she determines precisely which roles fit her vocal capabilities. *Nomen est omen:* it is perhaps no coincidence that, true to her name, Waltraute (*Götterdämmerung/Twilight of the Gods*) is one of Waltraud's first Wagnerian roles – a part she subsequently sings for over 30 years.

Her ability to alternate effortlessly between different vocal categories and contrasting characters in a single evening is demonstrated in 2002 in an unforgettable, unique, almost funky performance of *Die Walküre* at the Berlin Staatsoper, where a last-minute cancellation by a colleague results in Meier's stepping up and finessing *both* Sieglinde and Fricka!

Unquestionably one of her classic roles among Wagnerian heroines is Kundry, in which she achieves an ideal blending of singing, acting, and physical appearance. Additionally equipped with top notes like rocket flares, she exceeds all expectations in her sensational debut at Bayreuth in 1983. From then on she is the unrivaled premier performer of this part.

Yet none of her roles is ever alien to Meier, not even the mean Ortrud in *Lohengrin*. She need only »crawl« deep inside her heroines, she explains, to be fully able to empathise with them. Without such strong and sensitive intuition she would probably have fought a losing battle in her first *Tristan* at Bayreuth in 1993, where her director Heiner Müller offers her practically »no clues« to character interpretation. The geometrically outlined staging by Erich Wonder and the subtle effects of shifting lighting along with upscale, futuristic costumes create a powerful atmosphere. However, the greatest triumph – and also for the critics the »real stunner« – of this performance is Waltraud Meier: »The versatility of her voice is enormous. Every note is well calibrated and resonates freely. A better Isolde is, at present, hardly imaginable, owing as well to the exceptional intensity of her personality.« [1]

This Bayreuth *Tristan* focuses entirely on the impossibility of a fulfilled love. That is the reason why the second act does not take place in a cozy setting on a »bright, lovely summer night« as indicated in Wagner's libretto, but in an armory filled with mounted armor as a symbol of a weapon-obsessed male world. Audiences and press alike are divided on this interpretation which entirely aims at abstraction, and thus only rarely permits physical intimacy between the characters. In view of all that severity of staging, Waltraud Meier and Daniel Barenboim, above all, make sure that this most erotic, oscillating music ever written comes into its own. Several sparks are struck between stage and orchestra pit. »We are like hand and glove, I just don't know who is who«, Barenboim is quoted as saying after Waltraud Meier and he completed so many masterly performances together. Those words offer fond and fitting testimony to their longstanding close and fruitful artistic partnership.

For seventeen years Waltraud Meier makes Bayreuth Festival history as Kundry, Isolde and Waltraute. Then comes the breach. Her differences with Wolfgang Wagner stem from the strict compulsory attendance at rehearsals: since Meier is under contract for another role in Munich, she asks for a leave of absence for a few days, but Wagner does not want to make an exception.

As Sieglinde in a new *Ring* production, conducted by Giuseppe Sinopoli, Waltraud Meier bids farewell to Bayreuth in 2000. However, this rift merits only a marginal note since they are both soon »reconciled«. She counts among »the best of her life« those many years spent in Bayreuth with such »wonderful colleagues« as if »within a family circle.«

Among all her *Tristan* directors the singer singles out Patrice Chéreau, whose subtle psychological production make its debut in 2007 at La Scala in Milan, once again with Daniel Barenboim as conductor. Meier is delighted with »his way of portraying human destinies«, and grateful that unlike so many other directors he weighs every phrase and thinks right through to the end »the interaction between the characters on stage.«

Consequently she has the opportunity to illuminate the finest nuances of shifting emotions within this complex character: despair, vengefulness, desire, death wish.

The public and press alike celebrate her achievement. The *FAZ* critic goes wild over this Waltraud Meier who fashions an Isolde »still delightfully impetuous, yet clearly articulated and with secure intonation«. She is particularly striking at the moment in the first act, when Tristan and Isolde »find themselves drawn to each other, are fused in passion, and finally are violently sundered by Brangäne.« [2]

Waltraud Meier never performs the role of Brünnhilde. It would presumably require her to depart from her traditional mezzo range – something not to be recommended. Still, she takes up the challenge of singing Brünnhilde's concluding scene in *Götterdämmerung* on a Wagner CD, which by all accounts is simply splendid. But the role of her life is, and is forever, Isolde.

Nina Stemme, *11. Mai 1963 in Stockholm

Seit ihrer Isolde in Bayreuth gilt sie zu Recht als eine der größten Wagnersängerinnen ihrer Generation. Nina Stemme ist 2005 das einsame Glanzlicht der Festspiel-Produktion unter der Regie von Christoph Marthaler, die mit einem sterilen Ambiente und einer steif anmutenden Personenregie enttäuscht.

Als eine »Anti-Liebesutopie« hat ein Kritiker [1] diesen *Tristan* treffend beschrieben, entwickeln doch die Liebenden seltsame Neurosen aber keine Leidenschaft. Sie gestehen sich ihre Gefühle, ohne sich anzusehen, nie kommen sie richtig zusammen.

Zumindest aber glüht die Musik. Stemmes Sopran strahlt und funkelt in allen Lagen, mühelos steigert sie sich in ekstatische Ausbrüche, macht aber auch subtile Zwischentöne hör- und erlebbar. Entsprechend wird sie auch von Publikum und Presse gefeiert: »Ihr stimmlicher Höhenflug während des *Liebestods* war phänomenal und ließ die kalte Leichenhallen-Atmosphäre von Tristans Burg Kareol beinahe vergessen«, schreibt etwa *Der Spiegel*. [2]

Nina Stemme erarbeitet mit führenden Regisseuren ihrer Zeit unterschiedliche packende Psychogramme der Isolde, wobei sich die Figur mit der Entwicklung der Stimme verändert. Ihre erste, mit königlichen Insignien ausgestattete Isolde in einer Inszenierung von Nikolaus Lehnhoff in Glyndebourne 2003 erscheint noch sehr mädchenhaft, verletzbar und lyrisch. Bei ihren späteren Isolden nehmen Wut, gar Zynismus im ersten Akt größeren Raum ein.

Als sehr dankbar erweist sich 2008 die Inszenierung von Claus Guth in Zürich, die sich über weite Strecken überzeugend an der Entstehungsgeschichte des Musikdramas orientiert. Unübersehbar spiegelt sich im *Tristan* Richard Wagners eigene Geschichte einer verbotenen tragischen Liebe: Es war die künstlerisch-literarisch begabte Mathilde Wesendonck, die er anbetete. Sie inspirierte ihn zu seinem *Tristan*. Die junge Muse schwärmte ihrerseits schon für Richard Wagner, kaum dass sie ihn 1852 in Zürich kennen lernte, stellte aber ihr privates Glück hinter ihre familiären Pflichten und bürgerliche Moralvorstellungen zurück. Eine Scheidung von ihrem vermögenden Ehemann zog Mathilde nie in Betracht. – Zum Leidwesen Wagners. Wäre es nach ihm gegangen, hätte er ohne große Schuldgefühle seine Ehefrau Minna verlassen. Er fühlte sich sogar als Opfer dieser komplizierten Affäre. Dabei zeigten sich die Ehepartner der Liebenden lange Zeit gleichermaßen nachsichtig. Vor allem Otto Wesendonck, der Wagner sehr verehrte, sah über die außereheliche Liebe hinweg, förderte den Komponisten generös und ging als ein großzügiger Freund als der betrogene König Marke in den *Tristan* ein. Auch unterdrückte Minna Wagner lange Zeit ihre Eifersucht, bis die Situation für sie schließlich so unerträglich wurde, dass sie einen Skandal entfachte.

Diese komplexen Beziehungsstrukturen spiegeln sich in Guths Regiearbeit wider, die bei alledem mit Bildern von Schönheit und Poesie beeindruckt.

Zur Premiere wird Stemme abermals groß gefeiert: »Sie singt eine fulminante Isolde von derzeit konkurrenzloser Hochdramatik in dieser Partie. Und sie spielt eine der schönsten Isolden, nicht zuletzt dank der schönen Kostüme Christian Schmidts«, schwärmt der Wagner-kenner Dieter David Scholz. [3]

In dem großartigen konzertanten, auf CD aufgezeichneten Berliner Wagnerzyklus unter Marek Janowski stellt sie diese Qualitäten vier Jahre später wieder unter Beweis. Für Stemme ist es bereits die zweite Gesamtaufnahme des *Tristans*, die erste an der Seite von Placido Domingo datiert aus dem Jahr 2005.

Ihre Gesangsausbildung absolviert Nina Stemme zunächst neben einem Studium der Volks- und Betriebswirtschaft. Ihr Weg aber führt schnell steil nach oben. 1993 gewinnt sie einen ersten Preis im Placido-Domingo-Wettbewerb, bereits ein Jahr später debütiert sie bei den Bayreuther Festspielen als Freia im *Rheingold* unter James Levine. Schon wenige Wochen nach ihrem Rollendebüt als Senta im Jahr 2000 in Antwerpen wollen die Festspiele in Glyndebourne sie als Isolde verpflichten.

Von der legendären Birgit Nilsson erhält sie manch wertvollen fachlichen Rat, aber Unterricht nimmt sie nicht bei ihr, was sie rückblickend bedauert. Sie fühlte sich damals einfach nicht reif genug.

Lange ist sich Nina Stemme unsicher, ob sie auch die Brünnhilde in ihr Repertoire aufnehmen soll. Die Sieglinde, die sie immer wieder gern und oft an unterschiedlichen Bühnen verkörpert, steht ihr charakterlich als uneingeschränkt unschuldige, positive Figur deutlich näher. – Andererseits: »Welche weiteren Partien empfehlen sich einer Interpretin, deren Stimme sich ins Dramatische entwickelt, nach der Isolde?«

Als sie 2010 in Mailand in dem neuen *Ring* unter Daniel Barenboim als *Walküre* große Triumphe feiert, hat sie bereits einen ersten kompletten *Ring*-Zyklus in San Francisco unter Donald Runnicles sehr respektabel bewältigt.

Die Inszenierung von Guy Cassiers an der Scala aber enttäuscht. Der Belgier kümmert sich kaum um die Psychologie der Figuren und lässt die Sänger weite Strecken allein. Zumindest aber zeugen die außergewöhnlichen, majestätischen Designerkostüme, entworfen von Tim van Steenbergen, von Raffinesse. In einer androgyn anmutenden Kreation, halb Hose, halb Rock, und mit schulterfreiem Oberteil, wirkt Nina Stemmes Brünnhilde jugendlich, stolz, selbstbewusst und begehrlich, dabei auch allemal bodenständig in ihren Entscheidungen.

Vor allem aber in musikalischer Sicht ist die Schwedin eine Wucht. Von Jahr zu Jahr hat ihr Sopran an dramatischem Potenzial enorm gewonnen, besonders in den großen Dialogen mit Wotan und Siegmund führt sie ihre breit flutende, prächtige Stimme schlank bis in die Spitzen. Die Italiener ehren sie dafür mit dem Kritikerpreis *Premio Abbati*.

Einen ebenso starken Eindruck hinterlässt die Interpretin im Jahr 2012 als Brünnhilde in der *Götterdämmerung* an der Bayerischen Staatsoper unter Kent Nagano. Mit ihrem starken Auftritt überzeugt sie auch die Presse. So schreibt zum Beispiel die *Süddeutsche Zeitung*: »In ihrem Solofinale läuft sie zur Höchstform auf. Ihre Ruhe und die voluminöse Stimme erlauben ihr eine faszinierende Liebesklage, die dem *Ring* einen weit würdigeren Abschluss beschert als es die hier versammelte Niedertracht verdient hätte.«[4]

Eine trefflichere Nachfolgerin ihrer berühmten schwedischen Landsfrauen Birgit Nilsson und Catarina Ligendza ließe sich kaum denken. Nina Stemme schürt Hoffnungen auf noch viele großartige Musiktheatererlebnisse.

Nina Stemme mit
Michelle Breedt (Brangäne, links),
Oper Zürich 2008

Nina Stemme als Brünnhilde, Bayerische Staatsoper 2012

Nina Stemme, *11th May 1963 in Stockholm

Ever since her Isolde in Bayreuth she is rightly considered one of the greatest Wagnerian singers of her generation. Nina Stemme is the only bright spot in the Festspiele production directed by Christoph Marthaler, which otherwise is a disappointment in its sterile staging and stiff style of directing.

One critic [1] aptly described this *Tristan* as an »romantic dystopia« since the lovers develop strange neuroses but no true passion. They confess their feelings without looking at each other, and they never really come together.

At least the music blazes. Stemme's soprano sparkles and shines in all ranges; she effortlessly escalates into ecstatic outbursts, but also makes subtle nuances audible and tangeable. She is accordingly celebrated by both audience and press alike: »Her vocal flight during the love-death was phenomenal and allowed one almost to forget the cold tomb-like atmosphere of Tristan's castle Kareol«, we read, for example, in *Der Spiegel*. [2]

Nina Stemme assembles with the leading directors of her time a variety of poignant psychological profiles of Isolde, whereby the character changes with her vocal development. Her first Isolde, who is fitted with royal trappings in Nikolaus Lehnhoff's production at Glyndebourne in 2003, appears still maidenly, vulnerable and lyrical. Her later Isoldes incorporate a greater range of ire, even cynicism, in the first act.

Claus Guth's 2008 production in Zurich happily proves to be convincingly focused for long stretches on the history of the origins of Wagner's musical drama. Richard Wagner's *Tristan* obviously reflects his own personal story of a forbidden tragic love, as he adored the artistically gifted and literary Mathilde Wesendonck. It was she who inspired his *Tristan*.

The young muse for her part doted on Richard Wagner when she met him in Zürich in 1852. However, she put her family responsibilities and society's views of morality above her personal happiness. She never considered a divorce from her wealthy husband – to Wagner's great sorrow: for his part, he would have abandoned his wife Minna without any great compunction, and indeed even saw himself as a victim in that complicated love affair. In the course of the affair the spouses were equally forbearing toward the lovers. Especially Otto Wesendonck, who greatly admired Wagner, overlooked the extramarital affair, supported the composer generously, and was received as a generous friend – much as the deceived King Marke in *Tristan*. Minna Wagner, too, suppressed her jealousy until the situation became so unbearable for her that she caused a scandal.

This complex network of relationships is reflected in Guth's directing which dazzles everyone with images of beauty and poetry.

Stemme is once again greeted with great acclaim at the premiere: »She sings a brilliant Isolde with an unrivaled degree of high drama in this part at this time. And she plays one of the most beautiful Isoldes, not least of all thanks to Christian Schmidt's beautiful costumes«, raves the Wagner authority Dieter David Scholz. [3]

Stemme again gives proof of these very qualities in the splendid cycle of Wagnerian operas in concert under Marek Janowski in 2012. Recorded on CD, it represents Stemme's second recording of *Tristan*: the first was in 2005, with Placido Domingo.

No sooner has Nina Stemme completed her vocal training together with her business and economics studies than her career immediately takes off. In 1993, she wins first prize in the Placido Domingo Competition. One year later she debuts at the Bayreuth Festival as Freia in Wagner's *Rheingold*, directed by James Levine. Just a few weeks after her debut in 2000 as Senta in *Der fliegende Holländer* (*The Flying Dutchman*) in Antwerp, the Glyndebourne Festival wants to engage her as Isolde.

She receives priceless professional advice from the legendary Birgit Nilsson, but does not take lessons with her – something she regrets in hindsight. At the time Stemme simply did not yet feel she had enough experience.

For a long time Stemme remains unsure whether she should also include Brünnhilde in her repertoire. She feels closer to Sieglinde, an innocent, completely positive role, which she often enjoys performing on various stages. On the other hand: »What other roles commend themselves to a singer whose voice, after Isolde, has developed in a dramatic direction?«

By the time she scores her great triumphs as Brünnhilde in *Die Walküre* in 2010 in Milan, conducted by Daniel Barenboim, she has already most respectably mastered her first complete *Ring* Cycle in San Francisco, conducted by Donald Runnicles. But the staging by Guy Cassiers at La Scala is a disappointment.

The Belgian cares little, if anything, about the p The Belgian cares little, if anything, about the psychology of the characters and leaves the singers alone for long stretches. At least Tim van Steenbergens' extraordinary and majestic costume designs show ingenuity. In an androgynous creation – half pants, half skirt, and strapless top – Stemme's Brünnhilde appears youthful, proud, confident and covetous while at the same time always grounded in her decisions.

Above all, in her musicality the Swede is stunning. Stemme's soprano has developed enormous dramatic potential year after year, particularly in the great dialogues with Wotan and Siegmund, in which her superb, broadly flooding voice rises to the highest peaks. In response, the Italians honour her with the critics' choice award, *Premio Abbiati*.

When Stemme performs Brünnhilde in *Götterdämmerung* (*Twilight of the Gods*) at the Bavarian State Opera in 2012 under Kent Nagano, the impact is just as powerful and her performance leaves the press utterly satisfied. For instance, the *Süddeutsche Zeitung* reports: »In the Immolation Scene she is at her best. Her tranquillity and her voluminous voice allow her to convey a fascinating love-lament, which gives the *Ring* a far worthier conclusion than all the assembled malice had merited.« [4]

One cannot imagine a more splendid successor to her famous Swedish compatriots Birgit Nilsson and Catarina Ligendza. Nina Stemme stirs up hopes for many magnificent operatic experiences yet to come.

Dank

Mein ganz besonderer Dank gilt meinem exzellenten Übersetzer Charles Scribner,
ohne den dieses Buch nicht zweisprachig vorliegen würde,
und Anne Marie Hanauer, die beim Übersetzen assistiert hat.

Für intensive Gespräche, die Bereitstellung von Materialien und Untersützung
vielfältiger Art danke ich folgenden Personen und Institutionen: Philipp Albrecht,
Philip Behrens, Dr. Gabriele Beinhorn, Ludmila Dvořáková, Lillian Fayer,
Dr. Gudrun Foettinger, Dame Gwyneth Jones, Dr. Christiane Lehnigk, Renate Liese,
Catarina Ligendza, Peter Ligendza, Waltraud Meier, Dr. Gabriele E. Meyer,
Ragnhild Nyhus, Deborah Polaski, Thomas Rakow, Bettina Raeder, Curt Scheiwe,
Jacqueline Schwarz, Karl Franz Schulter, Anja Silja, Peter Sommeregger,
Chris Inken Soppa, Swantje Steinbrink, Nina Stemme, Barbara Strawitz,
Christian Thielemann, Helmut Vetter sowie der Fachzeitschrift *Opernwelt*,
dem Fotoarchiv der Metropolitan Opera New York,
dem Flagstad Museum Oslo und vielen mehr …

Und: meiner Verlegerin Josefine Rosalski, ohne die es dieses Buch nicht geben
würde.

Acknowledgements

I wish especially to thank my excellent translator Charles Scribner,
without whom this book would not exist in two languages, and
Anne Marie Hanauer, who assisted him in the translation.

For the intensive conversations and for providing various materials and support,
I also wish to thank the following people and institutions: Philipp Albrecht,
Philip Behrens, Dr. Gabriele Beinhorn, Ludmila Dvořáková, Lillian Fayer, Dr. Gudrun
Foettinger, Dame Gwyneth Jones, Dr. Christiane Lehnigk, Renate Liese,
Catarina Ligendza, Peter Ligendza, Waltraud Meier, Dr. Gabriele E. Meyer,
Ragnhild Nyhus, Deborah Polaski, Thomas Rakow, Bettina Raeder, Curt Scheiwe,
Jacqueline Schwarz, Karl Franz Schulter, Anja Silja, Peter Sommeregger,
Chris Inken Soppa, Swantje Steinbrink, Nina Stemme, Barbara Strawitz,
Christian Thielemann, Helmut Vetter as well as the magazine *Opernwelt*,
the photo archives of the Metropolitan Opera,
the Flagstad museum in Oslo and many more ...

Finally: my editor Josefine Rosalski, without whom this book would not exist.

Anmerkungen

Frida Leider

1 Frida Leider. *Das war mein Teil*. S. 103
2 Ebda. S. 94
3 *Wiener Zeitung* vom 21. Juni 1932
4 Frida Leider. *Das war mein Teil*. S. 64
5 Ebda. S. 169

Kirsten Flagstad

1 Zitiert nach: Kirsten Flagstad: *The Flagstad Manuscript*. S. 83
2 Siehe Kirsten Flagstad. *The Flagstad Manuscript*. S. 81
3 Zitiert und frei übersetzt nach *The Flagstad Manuscript*. S. 49 f
4 Lawrence Gilman zitiert nach: Jürgen Kesting. *Die großen Sänger*. S. 881
5 Zitiert und frei übersetzt nach *The Flagstad Manuscript*. S. 246

Martha Mödl

1 Siehe Martha Mödl. *So war mein Weg*. S. 66
2 Aribert Reimann in einem persönlichen Nachruf auf Martha Mödl in der *Opernwelt*, 2/2002. S. 24
3 Martha Mödl im Gespräch mit Karl Schumann in der Sendung *Eine Heroine aus der Nähe* vom 2. Dezember 1984 im *Bayerischen Rundfunk*
4 Hans Heinz Stuckenschmidt in der *Neuen Zeitung* vom 31. Juli 1953
5 Zitiert nach Martha Mödl: *So war mein Weg*. S. 64
6 Astrid Varnay in ihrem persönlichen Nachruf in der *Opernwelt*, Berlin, 2/2002. S. 19

Astrid Varnay

1 Astrid Varnay. *Hab' mir's gelobt*. S. 216
2 Astrid Varnay im Interview mit Dieter David Scholz. *Mythos Primadonna*. S. 288
3 Astrid Varnay im Interview mit Monika Beer: »Man muss wissen, wann man aufhört.« In: Gondrom's *Festspielmagazin*, 1997. Herausgegeben von der Buchhandlung Gondrom, Bayreuth 1997, S. 10
4 Varnay. *Hab' mir's gelobt*. S. 291
5 K. H. Ruppel in der *Süddeutschen Zeitung* vom 11. August 1951

6   K. H. Ruppel in der *Süddeutschen Zeitung* vom 2. August 1954

7   Varnay. *Hab' mir's gelobt.* S. 151

Birgit Nilsson

1   Zitiert nach: Birgit Nilsson. *La Nilsson.* S. 250

2   Diese Textpassage existiert in zwei unterschiedlichen Fassungen: Interpretinnen jüngerer Generationen wie z. B. Catarina Ligendza oder Dame Gwyneth Jones singen alternativ *Der mir diese Liebe ins Herz gehaucht.* Beide Textfassungen basieren original auf Richard Wagners Vorlagen. In der Erstschrift des Textbuches (1852) dichtete Wagner zunächst *Der mir in's Herz/diese Liebe gehaucht.* Diese Fassung findet sich auch im Erstdruck von 1853 sowie in den Textbüchern von 1863 (1873) und den Gesammelten Schriften und Dichtungen von 1872.

3   Birgit Nilsson. *La Nilsson.* S. 358 f

4   *La Nilsson.* S. 103 f

5   *La Nilsson.* S. 104

6   Reinhold K. Peter im *Münchner Merkur* vom 2. August 1966

Ludmila Dvořáková

1   Klaus Adam in der Zeitschrift *Oper und Konzert.* München 2/ 1964, S. 13

2   Ernst Krause in der *Opernwelt,* 1/1965. S. 33

3   Theo Hertel in *Oper und Konzert,* 3. Jg. 8/1965, S. 22

4   Ernst Krause in der *Opernwelt,* 1/1965. S. 33

Gwyneth Jones

1   Ausführlich aufgezeichnet hat den Skandal der *Spiegel* in seiner Ausgabe vom 2. August 1976

2   Reinhard Baumgart in der *Zeit* vom 3. September 1980

Hildegard Behrens

1, 2, 3 Hildegard Behrens in dem TV-Porträt *Hildegard Behrens* von Eckhardt Schmidt. *Bayerischer Rundfunk* 2008

4   Reinhard Beuth in der *Welt* vom 10. Juni 1980

5   Zitiert nach: Dieter David Scholz. *Mythos Primadonna.* S. 22

6   Reinhard Beuth in der *Welt* vom 1. August 1983

7   Joachim Kaiser in den Ausgaben der *Süddeutschen Zeitung* vom 28.Juli 1983 und vom 30. Juli 1983

8   Beate Kayser in der *TZ* vom 30. Juli 1983

Catarina Ligendza

1 Norbert Miller in der *Süddeutschen Zeitung* vom 10. Oktober 1985
2 Joachim Kaiser in der *Süddeutschen Zeitung* vom 11. April 1980
3 Hans Heinz Stuckenschmidt in der *Neuen Zürcher Zeitung* vom 27./28.April 1980

Anja Silja

1 Anja Silja. *Die Sehnsucht nach dem Unerreichbaren*. S. 53
2 Ebda. S. 65
3 Diese Textpassage existiert in zwei unterschiedlichen Fassungen: Einige Interpretinnen wie z. B. Catarina Ligendza oder Dame Gwyneth Jones singen alternativ *Der mir diese Liebe ins Herz gehaucht*. Beide Textfassungen basieren original auf Richard Wagners Vorlagen. In der Erstschrift des Textbuches (1852) dichtete Wagner zunächst *Der mir in's Herz/diese Liebe gehaucht*. Diese Fassung findet sich auch im Erstdruck von 1853 sowie in den Textbüchern von 1863 (1873) und den Gesammelten Schriften und Dichtungen von 1872. In der Erstschrift der Partitur seiner *Walküre* (1855/56) formulierte Wagner daran angelehnt *Der diese Liebe mir ins Herz gehaucht*. Die Forschung vermutet, dass Wagner die Änderung in der seit 1945 verschollenen Reinschrift der Partitur (1856) vorgenommen hat, die ihrerseits die Vorlage für den Erstdruck der Partitur gewesen ist.
4 Zitiert nach: Anja Silja. *Die Sehnsucht nach dem Unerreichbaren*. S. 130

Deborah Polaski

1 Joachim Kaiser in der *Süddeutschen Zeitung* vom 3. August 1988
2 Jochen Breiholz in der *Welt* vom 18. April 2000
3 Klaus Geitel in der *Berliner Morgenpost* vom 18. April 2000

Waltraud Meier

1 Eckhard Roelcke in der *Zeit* vom 30. Juli 1993
2 Julia Spinola in der *Frankfurter Allgemeinen Zeitung* vom 10. Dezember 2007

Nina Stemme

1 Claus Spahn in der *Zeit* vom 28. Juli 2005
2 Werner Theurich im *Spiegel* vom 26. Juli 2005
3 Dieter David Scholz in seinen Rezensionen im *Südwestrundfunk* und im *Bayerischen Rundfunk* am 11. Dezember 2008
4 Reinhard Brembeck in der *Süddeutschen Zeitung* vom 2. Juli 2012

Notes

Frida Leider

1 Frida Leider, *Das war mein Teil*, p. 103
2 Ibid., p. 94
3 *Wiener Zeitung* (21 June 1932)
4 Frida Leider, *Das war mein Teil*, p. 64
5 Ibid., p. 169

Kirsten Flagstad

1 Quoted from Kirsten Flagstad, *The Flagstad Manuscript*, p. 83
2 See Kirsten Flagstad, *The Flagstad Manuscript*, p. 81
3 Quoted and loosely translated from *The Flagstad Manuscript*, p. 49 f
4 Lawrence Gilman quoted from Jürgen Kesting, *Die großen Sänger*, p. 881
5 Quoted and loosely translated from *The Flagstad Manuscript*, p. 246

Martha Mödl

1 See Martha Mödl, *So war mein Weg*, p. 66
2 Aribert Reimann in his memorial of Martha Mödl in *Opernwelt*, 2/2002, p. 24
3 Martha Mödl in conversation with Karl Schumann in the broadcast *Eine Heroine aus der Nähe* (2 Dezember 1984), *Bayerischer Rundfunk*
4 Hans Heinz Stuckenschmidt in *Neue Zeitung* (31 July 1953)
5 Quoted from Martha Mödl, *So war mein Weg.* p. 64
6 Astrid Varnay in her memorial of Mödl in *Opernwelt*, Berlin, 2/2002, p. 19

Astrid Varnay

1 Astrid Varnay, *Hab' mir's gelobt*, p. 216
2 Astrid Varnay in an interview with Dieter David Scholz, *Mythos Primadonna*, p. 288
3 Astrid Varnay in an interview with Monika Beer: »One must know when to call it a day.« In Gondrom's *Festspielmagazin* (published by Gondrom's bookstore), *Bayreuth*, 1997, p. 10
4 Varnay, *Hab' mir's gelobt*, p. 291
5 K. H. Ruppel in *Süddeutsche Zeitung* (11 August 1951)
6 K. H. Ruppel in *Süddeutsche Zeitung* (2 August 1954)
7 Varnay, *Hab' mir's gelobt*, p. 151

Birgit Nilsson

1 Quoted from Birgit Nilsson, *La Nilsson,* p. 250

2 This passage exists in two different versions: Sopranos of more recent generations, such as Catarina Ligendza or Dame Gwyneth Jones sing alternatively *Der mir diese Liebe ins Herz gehaucht* (verbatim *Who me this love in the heart breathed*). Both are based on Richard Wagner's original texts. In the first version of the libretto (1852) Wagner initially cast the verse *Der mir in's Herz/diese Liebe gehaucht* (*Who me in the heart/ this love breathed*). This wording is also included in the first printing of 1853 as well as in the libretto of 1863 (1873) and the *Collected Writings and Poems,* 1872.

3 Birgit Nilsson, *La Nilsson,* p. 358 f

4 *La Nilsson, p.* 103 f

5 *La Nilsson, p.* 104

6 Reinhold K. Peter in *Münchner Merkur* (2 August 1966)

Ludmila Dvořáková

1 Klaus Adam in the journal *Oper und Konzert,* München 2/1964, p. 13

2 Ernst Krause in *Opernwelt,* 1/1965, p. 33

3 Theo Hertel in *Oper und Konzert,* vol. 3, 8/1965, p. 22

4 Ernst Krause in *Opernwelt,* 1/1965, p. 33

Gwyneth Jones

1 The scandal was reported in depth by *Der Spiegel* (2 August 1976)

2 Reinhart Baumgart in *Die Zeit (*3 September 1980)

Hildegard Behrens

1, 2, 3 Hildegard Behrens in the TV documentary *Hildegard Behrens* by Eckhardt Schmidt, *Bayerischer Rundfunk* 2008

4 Reinhard Beuth in *Die Welt* (10 June 1980)

5 Quoted from Dieter David Scholz, *Mythos Primadonna,* p. 22

6 Reinhard Beuth in *Die Welt (*1 August 1983)

7 Joachim Kaiser in two issues of the journal *Süddeutsche Zeitung (*28 July 1933 and 30 July 1983)

8 Beate Kayser in *TZ* (30 July 1983)

Catarina Ligendza

1 Norbert Miller in *Süddeutsche Zeitung* (10 October 1985)

2 Joachim Kaiser in *Süddeutsche Zeitung* (11 April 1980)

3 Hans Heinz Stuckenschmidt in *Neue Zürcher Zeitung* (27/28 April 1980)

Anja Silja

1 Anja Silja, *Die Sehnsucht nach dem Unerreichbaren*, p. 53
2 Ibid., p. 65
3 This passage exists in two different versions: Several performers such as Catarina Ligendza and Dame Gwyneth Jones sing alternatively *Der mir diese Liebe ins Herz gehaucht* (literally: *Who me this love in the heart breathed*). Both texts are based on Richard Wagner's originals. In the first copy of the libretto (1852) Wagner initially cast the verse *Der mir in's Herz/diese Liebe gehaucht (literally: Who me in the heart/this love breathed)*. This wording is also found in the first printing of 1853 as well as in the libretto of 1863 (1873) and the *Collected Writings and Poems* in 1872. Subsequently Wagner rephrased it in the first draft of the musical score of *Die Walküre* (1855/56) as *Der diese Liebe mir ins Herz gehaucht (literally: Who this love me in the heart breathed)*. Scholars presume that Wagner made this alteration in the 1856 clean copy of the score (missing since 1945) which was in turn the basis for the score's first printing.
4 Quoted from Anja Silja, *Die Sehnsucht nach dem Unerreichbaren*, p. 130

Deborah Polaski

1 Joachim Kaiser in *Süddeutsche Zeitung* (3 August 1988)
2 Jochen Breiholz in *Die Welt* (18 April 2000)
3 Klaus Geitel in *Berliner Morgenpost* (18 April 2000)

Waltraud Meier

1 Eckhard Roelcke in *Die Zeit* (30 July 1993)
2 Julia Spinola in *Frankfurter Allgemeine Zeitung (1*0 December 2007)

Nina Stemme

1 Claus Spahn in *Die Zeit* (28 July 2005)
2 Werner Theurich in *Der Spiegel* (26 July 2005)
3 Dieter David Scholz in his reviews in *Südwestrundfunk* and in *Bayerischer Rundfunk* (11 December 2008)
4 Reinhard Brembeck in *Süddeutsche Zeitung* (2 July 2012)

Literaturnachweise / Bibliographical References

Frida Leider
Das war mein Teil. Erinnerungen einer Opernsängerin.
Henschel-Verlag. Berlin 1981

Kirsten Flagstad
The Flagstad Manuscript. An Autobiography.
Louis Leopold Bancolli (Hrsg.), G.P. Putnam's Sons, New York 1952

Martha Mödl
So war mein Weg. Gespräche mit Thomas Voigt.
Parthas Verlag, Berlin 1998

Astrid Varnay
Hab' mir's gelobt. 55 Jahre in fünf Akten.
Henschel Verlag, Berlin 1997

Birgit Nilsson
La Nilsson. Mein Leben für die Oper.
Fischer-Verlag, Frankfurt 1999

Anja Silja
Die Sehnsucht nach dem Unerreichbaren. Wege und Irrwege.
Parthas Verlag, Berlin 1999

Helen Traubel
St. Louis Woman.
Duell, Sloan and Pearce, New York 1959

Jens-Malte Fischer
Große Stimmen. Von Enrico Caruso bis Jessye Norman.
Suhrkamp Verlag, Frankfurt 1995

Jürgen Kesting
Die großen Sänger.
3 Bände, Claassen, Düsseldorf 1986

Dieter David Scholz
Mythos Primadonna/25 Diven widerlegen ein Klischee.
Parthas Verlag, Berlin 1999

Eva Rieger
Minna und Richard Wagner. Stationen einer Liebe.
Patmos Verlag, Düsseldorf und Zürich 2003

Richard Wagner
Werke, Schriften und Briefe. Herausgegeben von Sven Friedrich.
Digitale Ausgabe auf CD Rom, Directmedia, Berlin 2004

Personenregister / *Index of Persons*

Bildnachweise / Photo Credits

Buchumschlag Titel
Kirsten Flagstad als Brünnhilde, Paramount Studios, Hollywood, 1937: Archiv des Kirsten Flagstad Museums, Oslo

Buchumschlag Innenseite
Szenenfoto mit Kirsten Flagstad als Brünnhilde, Metropolitan Opera, New York, undatiert: Archiv des Kirsten Flagstad Museums, Oslo. Porträtfoto der Autorin: Studio Ideal, Berlin

Einleitung:
Helen Traubel als Isolde. New York, 1942: Fotoarchiv der Metropolitan Opera. Malvina und Ludwig Schnorr von Carolsfeld als Tristan und Isolde: historische Abbildung um 1865. Gwyneth Jones als Malvina, Foto: Karl-Heinz Lammel. Amalie Materna als Brünnhilde: Historische Abbildung um 1876

Frida Leider
Als Brünnhilde, Bayreuther Festspiele 1927; als Isolde, Berliner Staatsoper, ca. 1937: Archiv der Frida Leider Gesellschaft (Peter Sommeregger)

Kirsten Flagstad
Als Brünnhilde, Metropolitan Opera New York, 1935; als Isolde, Rollendebüt an der Metropolitan Opera, New York, 6. Februar 1935: Archiv des Kirsten Flagstad Museums, Oslo

Martha Mödl
Als Kundry, Debüt zur Eröffnung der Bayreuther Festspiele 1951: Nationalarchiv der Richard-Wagner-Stiftung, Bayreuth – Zustifter Wolfgang Wagner. Als Isolde, Theater an der Wien, 12.06.1954, Foto: Lillian Fayer

Astrid Varnay
Als Isolde, Metropolitan Opera, New York, 1945: Fotoarchiv der Metropolitan Opera. Als Brünnhilde, Bayreuther Festspiele 1964: Nationalarchiv der Richard-Wagner-Stiftung, Bayreuth – Zustifter Wolfgang Wagner

Birgit Nilsson
Als Isolde, Metropolitan Opera, New York, 1959: Fotoarchiv der Metropolitan Opera. Birgit Nilsson (Brünnhilde) und Gottlob Frick (Hagen) in der Götterdämmerung, Bayreuther Fest-

spiele 1962: Nationalarchiv der Richard-Wagner-Stiftung, Bayreuth – Zustifter Wolfgang Wagner

Ludmila Dvořáková
Als Brünnhilde, Bayreuther Festspiele 1967: Nationalarchiv der Richard-Wagner-Stiftung, Bayreuth – Zustifter Wolfgang Wagner. Als Isolde, Metropolitan Opera, New York, 1967: Fotoarchiv der Metropolitan Opera

Dame Gwyneth Jones
Als Brünnhilde in *Siegfried*, Bayreuther Festspiele 1977. Privatarchiv Dame Gwyneth Jones. Szene aus der Götterdämmerung mit Dame Gwyneth Jones (Brünnhilde), Manfred Jung (Siegfried, rechts) und Karl Ridderbusch (Hagen), Bayreuther Festspiele 1977. Privatarchiv Dame Gwyneth Jones

Hildegard Behrens
Als Brünnhilde, Metropolitan Opera New York,1983: Fotoarchiv der Metropolitan Opera. Als Isolde, Metropolitan Opera, New York, 1983: Fotoarchiv der Metropolitan Opera

Catarina Ligendza
Probenfoto mit Wolfgang Wagner. Bayreuther Festspiele, undatiert; als Isolde mit Yvonne Minton (Brangäne), Bayreuther Festspiele 1974, beide Fotos: Privatarchiv Catarina Ligendza

Anja Silja
Als Elisabeth im *Tannhäuser*, Bayreuther Festspiele 1962: Privatarchiv Anja Silja. Als Brünnhilde mit George London in der *Walküre*, Oper Köln 1963: Privatarchiv Anja Silja

Deborah Polaski
Als Brünnhilde, Bayreuther Festspiele 1995: Nationalarchiv der Richard-Wagner-Stiftung, Bayreuth – Zustifter Wolfgang Wagner. Als Isolde, Staatsoper Berlin, 2000, Foto: Monika Rittershaus

Waltraud Meier
Szene aus *Tristan und Isolde* mit Waltraud Meier (Isolde), Siegfried Jerusalem (Tristan) und Falk Struckmann (Kurwenal, hinten), Bayreuther Festspiele 1999: Nationalarchiv der Richard-Wagner-Stiftung, Bayreuth – Zustifter Wolfgang Wagner. Als Isolde, Teatro alla Scala, Mailand 2007, Foto: Brescia/ Amisano © Teatro alla Scala

Nina Stemme
Als Isolde mit Michelle Breedt (Brangäne), Oper Zürich 2008, Foto: Susanne Schwiertz. Als Brünnhilde, Bayerische Staatsoper 2012, Foto: Wilfried Hösl

In einzelnen Fällen konnten die Inhaber der Rechte an den reproduzierten Fotos nicht ausfindig gemacht werden. Der Verlag bittet, ihm bestehende Ansprüche mitzuteilen.

In some individual cases the owners of the photograph reproduction rights could not be traced. The publishing house requests that any remaining permissions be addressed to them directly.